LIFE IS FOR

LIFE IS FOR EVERYONE

A Source Book for Church Services

John C Sharp
and
John Wilson

THE SAINT ANDREW PRESS
EDINBURGH

First published in 1988 by
THE SAINT ANDREW PRESS
121 George Street, Edinburgh

British Library Cataloguing in Publication Data
Sharp, John C.
  Life is for everyone.
  1. Christian drama   2. Liturgical drama
  I. Title   II. Wilson, John, 1926-
  264   BV10.2

ISBN 0-7152-0613-3

Scripture quotations in this publication (unless marked otherwise)
are from the Holy Bible New International Version.
Copyright © 1973, 1978, 1984 International Bible Society.
Published by Hodder & Stoughton

*The Publisher acknowledges financial assistance from
The Drummond Trust towards the publication of this volume.*

Typeset by St. George Typesetting, Redruth, Cornwall

Printed in Great Britain by Bell and Bain Ltd, Glasgow

Contents

Introduction

This is a source book of scripts which can be used in different ways and in a wide variety of situations. They can be used at formal church services, special meetings, or school assemblies. They can be used individually or a selection of scripts could fit into part of a service. A complete programme can be built up by using a number of scripts and presenting them with congregational singing and musical interludes.

Apart from a few poems, which we have attributed to the authors, all the scripts are our own work. They are an attempt to present old truths in new ways and to use contemporary techniques in proclaiming the old — yet ever relevant — Gospel. They come from much thought, practice and experimentation.

These scripts are not meant to replace the sermon or devalue the faithful preaching of the word of God. We hold unreservedly to that word and know that God has ordained preaching as a means of proclaiming Jesus Christ as Saviour and Lord. But we believe that formal preaching is not the only way we can call people to repent and turn to Christ in faith.

We must seek to communicate to modern man in a contemporary way. Ours is a fragmented culture. The mass media of our age — newspapers, radio, television — seem designed to impress and to move people emotionally rather than to instruct and inform them. Everything is short and snappy, geared to be interesting and entertaining rather than making demands upon the intellect. So we have to learn how to reach men and women today in our broken age.

As the Scriptures should be our guide in all things we can learn from them how to communicate. The Bible is not a logical treatise on systematic theology but contains many different forms of verbal and dramatic communication. God, in speaking to us in his word, uses historical narrative, poetry, parables, stories, epigrams, and other types of literary forms. It is not wrong to use these literary techniques today and this is what we have tried to do in these scripts.

All Christians should be concerned with good communications and three things must be said about Christian communication. First, it is the message that is important, not the messengers. Our task is to present Jesus Christ who alone is the way, the truth and the life. So we should not draw attention to ourselves by trying to show how clever we are. Second, all Christian witness is only truly effective when God's spirit is in the message and the messengers. Whatever means we use must be in complete dependence upon the Lord. Without him we can do nothing. Third, no Christian communication can be truly adequate unless prayer lies behind it. In all things we must pray. But prayerful dependence upon the Lord does not mean we can be lazy in our preparation and presentation. Only our very best should be done for our Lord.

How to use this Book

We hope that those using these scripts will not be afraid to experiment and therefore we do not want to dictate how they should be used. We have, for convenience sake, divided the scripts into sections around the general theme of Life.

The first two sections deal with the basic aspects of life and many of the misconceptions and illusions people have about life. The third section presents God and the Gospel as the only source of real life. A fourth section deals with our response to God's offer of life in Jesus Christ. The last two sections are concerned with the Christian life and the resources God provides for living an abundant life.

Those using the book should not slavishly follow this particular order of scripts. For example, in the first section we have a script about the material cost of the commercialised Christmas, while in the third section we have a script about the real cost of Christmas to our Lord. These could be used effectively in that order but that order could be reversed, or the scripts used separately, to suit a particular occasion or audience. We want to leave it to those using the book to decide not only what scripts to use but the best order in which to use them.

Letters and Testimonies obviously should be read by one person but generally each script should be read by two, three or more voices with each taking alternate lines or paragraphs. As presentation is important, groups using the scripts should rehearse if possible. Careful consideration should be given to where each speaker should stand and how each script should be presented, the tone of voice used and the tempo at which it should be read.

Scripts should be adapted to suit local conditions and the particular audience at which they are aimed. Some scripts may require occasional updating. Some can be made more effective with the use of visual aids or spoken against a background of appropriate music.

In all things they should be used prayerfully and imaginatively.

I
WHAT IS LIFE?

1   What is Life?

What is life?
It is birth,
Childhood,
Adolescence,
Maturity,
Old age,
And death.
Life is a mist that appears for a little — and vanishes.
It is a breath,
A sigh,
A cry,
A laugh,
A tear,
An endless struggle.
It is eating,
Drinking,
Working,
Sleeping,
Playing.
What is life?
It is physical.
And yet it is also spiritual.
It is a creation of God.
Dependent on God.
Yet spoiled by sin.
But it can be re-created by God.
And real life involves
Faith,
Worship,
Knowing God,

Walking with God,
Having communion with God.
In him we live and move and have our being.
In him we live.
He is the origin of life.
In him we move.
He is the continuance of life.
In him we have our being.
He is the goal of life.

2   What is a Family?

What is a family?
It's a collection of people brought about by an accident of
birth.
It's people who happen to be related to one another.
It's a group of people who live together.
Who occasionally see one another.
Occasionally eat together.
Occasionally talk together.
Occasionally watch television together.
Occasionally go places together.
A family is a group of people who regularly quarrel.
About where to go together.
About which TV channel to watch.
About which records to play.
About who will take the dog out.
About pocket money.
About having to wait for the bathroom.
A family is a group of people who never go on holiday
together.
Who never go to church together.
Who never play together.

Who never pray together.
A modern family seems to be a group of people who are
never together.
Is this really a family?

3   What is Work?

What is work?
It's just a job.
A means of getting money.
A livelihood.
It's usually pretty dull.
Boring,
Monotonous.
It can be just shoving a pencil.
Filling in forms.
Battering a typewriter.
Tending a machine.
Serving customers who are always complaining.
Then there is work for which you are not paid.
Washing dishes,
Washing clothes,
Washing the car,
Keeping the house clean,
Cooking for a family,
Gardening.
Yes — and some of these things can be quite satisfying.
I suppose work is a necessary evil.
But it can be a calling.
The humblest forms of work can be fulfilling.
Achieving,
Creative,
Worthwhile.

Yes — Jesus was a carpenter.
Paul was a tentmaker.
David was a shepherd.
John was a fisherman.
What is work?
A means of serving others.
Jesus washed the disciples' feet.
He kindled a fire.
Cooked a breakfast.
Jesus worked for others.
How do you see work?

4   What is Leisure?

What is leisure?
It's digging the garden.
Knitting.
Reading.
Watching television.
Walking.
Swimming.
Jogging.
Games.
Games to play and games to watch.
Hobbies.
Golf.
Bowls.
Crosswords.
Tiddlywinks.
Do-it-yourself.
Leisure can be passive — where we sit and do nothing.
Leisure can be active — where we do things.
Leisure can be creative — where we make things.

So do you think leisure is self-centred?
It shouldn't be — because it should include
Doing things for others.
Visiting the sick.
Giving time to the lonely.
Helping others.
Hospitality.
And leisure should include the re-creation of the soul.
How do you use your leisure?

5 Television

Television is for entertainment,
For education,
For information,
It is claimed to be a window on the world.
And yet through this window we see murders,
Violence,
Adultery.
A window on the world?
What do you see through your window?
What is television doing to us?
We see famine in Africa.
Violence in Northern Ireland.
Refugees in Asia.
And then watch the latest variety or quiz show.
Does this not numb our sensitivity?
Violence and variety are reduced to the same level.
A show for our entertainment!
Television can be good.
But it can also mislead us.
Brainwash,
Give us new values,

False values.
What is television doing to you?
Do you switch off your mind when you switch on the set?

6   What Men Think of Life

J M Barrie said: 'Life is like a cup of tea; the more heartily we drink the sooner we reach the dregs.'

Bertrand Russell said: 'Real life, to most men, is a long second best, a perpetual compromise between the ideal and the possible.'

John Masefield said: 'Life is a long headache in a noisy street.'

Mahatma Ghandi said: 'If you want to understand the life of Western man you must realise that, in spite of what he says in his church or creed, money is his god.'

T S Eliot said: 'We are the straw men,
                The hollow men ...
                Where is the life we have lost in living?'

G K Chesterton said: 'Whatever else is true of the life of man, it is certainly true that man is not what he was meant to be.'

Dag Hammarskjold said: 'What I ask is absurd — that life shall have a meaning. What I strive for is impossible — that my life shall acquire a meaning.'

Henry Thoreau said: 'The mass of men lead lives of quiet desperation.'

George Santayana said: 'Life is not a spectacle or a feast, it is a predicament.'

Søren Kierkegaard said: 'Life can only be understood backwards; but is must be lived forwards.'

Someone said: 'When a person puts his best foot forward he gets it stepped on — that's life.'

Mark Twain said: 'Life would be infinitely happier if we could only be born at the age of 80 and gradually approach 18.'

A philosopher said: 'What the meaning of human life may be I don't know; I incline to suspect that it has none.'

Martin Esslin said: 'The dignity of man lies in his ability to face reality in all its meaninglessness.'

Albert Einstein said: 'The man who regards his own life and that of his fellow creatures as meaningless is not merely unhappy but hardly fit for life.'

Sigmund Freud/said: 'The good of all life is death.'

But Jesus said: 'I am the resurrection and the life. He who believes in me will live, even though he dies.'

7   Creeds

All men have creeds which express their deepest beliefs and guide their actions. What are the creeds of those who would shape the world without God?

There is the creed of the politician who would rule without God.

I believe in the Party; the source of all political wisdom and the maker of the perfect society on earth; and in the activists, sons and daughters of the Party who will bring all things about. I believe in the sovereignty of the people — the electors who can express their will through the Party.

And I believe in good government, which is the Party taking control of all things, serving the people by ruling the people. I believe in the brotherhood of all Party members; and in the perfect society that can come through the will of the Party. I have faith in the Party, hope in the Party, and eternally love the Party.

I believe in the future when all poverty, crime, illness and disaster can be abolished, in, through and by the Party.

We have the creed of the economist who would organise all things without God.

I believe in economics and the almighty power of money; and in the freedom of market forces, manipulated by government intervention.

I believe in sound money as the basis of sound government; and in the free society with freedom to create wealth and amass riches. I believe in enterprise and investment; in tariff agreements and a healthy balance of payments.

I believe in money being the measure of all things, and in the good life where money can satisfy all human demands.

Then there is the creed of the technologist who would exclude God from his thoughts.

I believe in science, almighty, analyser and creator of all things; and in technology as its only begotten son who is lord of life today. Technology can make all things new: all sickness and crime, trouble and strife, can be abolished through the intelligent application of technology. Death can be abolished, the universe explored, the stars conquered and mankind made immortal.

I believe in gadgets and technical things; in a techno-elite to rule all things; and in the microchip and computer to replace the fallibility of man.

I believe in the life everlasting created and made visible through, in and by technology.

Then there is the creed of the educationalist who mocks the idea that the fear of the Lord is the beginning of wisdom.

I believe in education, almighty, creator of the good life, and in an educational elite as the only children worthy of a civilised society.

I believe in that new society which will come to pass when all ignorance and illiteracy have been banished. I believe in comprehensive education: social, moral and political education; the teaching of all subjects except religion which can only be the manipulation of the false values of the past.

I believe in education as the answer to all human problems; in learning as the source of salvation, and human wisdom as the only hope for mankind.

Then we have the creed of the businessman who seeks to ignore God.

I believe in capital, almighty, maker of wealth, and in profit as the only worthy son.

I believe in the sovereignty of the shareholder. I believe in market forces for deciding wages and conditions; in advertising to create demand; in expansion and multi-nationals; in competition and conglomerates.

I believe in management techniques applied to all of life, and that only business practice and procedure makes a good society and life for men.

And we have the creed of the agnostic trade unionist.

I believe in the workers and in the dignity of labour as the only begotten son.

I believe in the solidarity of the workers and the brotherhood of all men; except, of course, scabs, blacklegs and those who refuse to join. I believe in the equality of all men and proper differentials in wages; in pay rises and shorter hours and the divine right to strike.

I believe in the ultimate triumph of the proletariat when the perfect society will come to pass with the workers of the world uniting.

8   What We have done with Our World — Dominion

What have we done to our world?
We have conquered it.
Explored the continents.
Ascended to the heavens.
Gone to the moon.
And descended to the depths of the ocean.
We have made the deserts flourish as a rose.

And cut continents in half.
By the Panama Canal.
The Suez Canal.
We have built roads all round the world.
With car and train vast distances are covered quickly.
By plane we can travel faster than sound.
By radio we can speak to the whole world.
And with television have the whole world brought into
   our living room.
We have created wealth.
By mining the earth's resources.
Farming the land.
Harvesting the ocean.
And turning these resources of earth, land and sea into
   commodities for our use.
Computers and microchip technology have taken much of
   drudgery out of work.
By electricity we have turned night into day.
And medical technology has conquered many diseases.
Mankind has harvested the power of the wind.
The power of steam.
The power of tide and wave.
The power of electricity.
And even the power of the atom.
Yes — man can use the power of the atom!

9   What We have done with Our World — Destruction

In the beginning God created the heavens and the earth,
   and God saw that it was very good.
But what have we done with the world?

We have changed our environment.
Polluted it.
Concreted it over.
Poisoned the rivers.
Oiled the seas and the beaches.
Put lead in the air for children to breathe.
We have caused our hedgerows to disappear.
And killed off wildlife.
Torn down the great forests.
And created deserts.
We have bombarded our ears with a cacophony of sound.
And blinded our eyes with flashing lights.
We have raped the world's resources.
On the assumption that there is no tomorrow.
What have we done with the world?
We have torn it apart in war and violence.
And ravished the earth.
With high explosive.
Atomic bombs.
Hydrogen bombs.
In the beginning God created the heavens and the earth,
     and God saw that it was very good.
But who made boundaries and barriers?
Who erects custom posts?
And who appoints frontier guards?
Who prints passports and issues visas?
Who is it that fences off the hills?
Walls the fields?
Decrees that certain rivers are
Private property?
Who is it that forbids us to walk on the grass?
That will not allow us to wander among the trees?
And who created out of nothing such terms as
Private?
Prohibited?
Banned?

Secret?
Segregate?
Exclusive?
No admittance?
Keep out?
Keep off?
Keep away?
And who decided trees should be made into crosses?
And atoms into explosives?
In the beginning God,
And in the end man created the world. And behold he
    saw that it was very bad.

10   What's Wrong with the World?

What's wrong with the world?
International tension.
Economic recession.
Inflation.
Unemployment.
Lack of resources.
Poverty.
Pollution.
Overpopulation.
Urbanisation.
Violence.
Hate.
Greed.
Envy.
Sin.

Listen to what some intellectuals have said:

Karl Marx said: 'The ''increasing value'' of the world of

things proceeds in direct proportion to the devaluation of the world of men.'

Arthur Koestler said: 'To dwell on the glories of man and ignore the symptoms of his possible insanity is not a sign of optimism but of ostrichism.'

Winston Churchill said: 'The heart of the problem of man is the problem of the heart of man.'

Eugène Ionesco said: 'Let us look about us. The world has lost its direction. No doubt, we have no shortage of ideologies of the most diverse kinds. But they lead nowhere.'

Hans Rookmaaker said: 'Man is plastic ... Plastic, the supreme product of technocracy ... our gadgets, instead of making man free they enslave him. Instead of bringing life they bring death.'

George Orwell said: 'If you want a picture of the future, imagine a boot stamping on a human face — forever.'

Paul said: 'For all have sinned and fall short of the glory of God.'

When G K Chesterton was asked to write on what is wrong with the world, he replied: 'Dear Sir, I am, yours sincerely, G K Chesterton.'

11　Materialism

Jesus said: 'A man's life does not consist in the abundance of his possessions.' (Luke 12:15)

Modern man says: Don't you believe it.
A man's life consists of:
What he is worth.
His bank balance.
The size of his house.
And its furnishings.
All the necessities, such as,
A colour television.
With portable ones for other rooms.
A video.
A hi-fi.
A home computer.
A holiday home.
Holidays abroad — twice a year.

Jesus said: 'A man's life does not consist in the abundance of his possessions.'

Modern man says: Don't you believe it.
The philosophy behind our society is:
Create more desire.
Thou shalt consume.
Thou shalt spend.
Thou shalt buy.
Thou shalt throw away.
And thou shalt buy again.
And again.
And again.

Jesus said: 'A man's life does not consist in the abundance of his possessions.'

Modern man says: A man's life consists of things.

12   Humanist Dialogue

One of the changes today is a general turning away from the Bible. As Christians we believe in God, Jesus and the Bible. But many do not. They say the Bible is an interesting book full of interesting stories that happened long, long ago. They say people can't believe the Bible today. The Bible is about God creating the world, loving the world, doing miraculous things and even sending his son into the world. They say people can't believe that today. The story of Jesus: born in a stable, angels and shepherds, wise men and big bad Herod — they say that's the stuff that fairy tales are made of. Then the life of Jesus: miracles and healings, his death and resurrection — they say it's a nice story, but romantic, the stuff of myths and legends. It's nothing to do with the facts of history; the facts of life; the facts of the 20th century. So they say.

After all, this is the 20th century.
    The age of science and technology.
The age of intelligence and achievement.
    The age of progress.
    Like atom bombs, terrorism, vandalism, muggings.
Now you take the Bible.
    No, you keep it, I don't want it. Nobody wants the Bible today.
That's what I mean. Nobody believes the Bible today.

I believe it.

It's full of incredible stories.

It even says that God made the world. Everybody knows that it began with a big bang and just evolved.

Science has certainly put the Bible in its place.

For one thing, miracles don't happen.

Of course not; science has proved that miracles don't — can't — happen.

But science has not proved God can't do miracles.

Of course, don't get me wrong — I believe Jesus was a good man.

He certainly gave a good example for people to follow.

And he was a good teacher.

Yes, he said a lot of very good and interesting things.

Like saying he was God and Lord of all.

But he lived long, long ago.

And he's dead.

There is no proof that he's alive today.

I was speaking to him a little while ago.

What do you make of this idea that he was supposed to have risen from the dead?

No one rises from the dead. When you're dead you're dead and that's the end of it.

No — it just doesn't happen.

I think what the resurrection means is that his spirit, his teaching, lives on.

Certainly his dead body couldn't have come alive again.

Yet after the resurrection he cooked breakfast and ate a meal with his disciples.

No — the resurrection stories are just the illusions of a few simple folk.

Paul says 500 saw the risen Lord at the same time.

In fact all the stories of the Bible are far-fetched.

It's mind-blowing to think of them.

What about the Red Sea — the waters parting to let the people walk across?

Then that bush that was supposed to be burning without being burned up?

Manna coming down from heaven?

And what about a man supposed to be born of a virgin?

And being able to turn water into wine?

Feeding thousands with a little boy's packed lunch?

Walking on water?

No one could do these things.

God did.

No — this is the 20th century:

The age of science and technology.

The age of achievement and progress.

The age of sin and despair.

No one can believe the Bible today.

I do.

And no one can believe the Gospels today.

So you say.

NB: Lines in italics should be spoken by a third voice.

13   The Cost of Christmas

Christmas is an expensive time, isn't it? It's money, money, money for everything. Think of the cost of Christmas.

This is going to be the dearest Christmas ever.

Have you seen the price of Christmas trees? It's terrible!

What about fairy lights? I paid almost £3.00 for a small set of coloured lights.

You can pay up to £2.00 for six baubles to hang on a tree.

What about decorations? You can pay pounds for strips of coloured paper.

And almost a pound for a small bunch of holly.

One thing — I'm cutting down on the number of Christmas cards I'm sending.

It's not just the price of cards — it's the cost of postage.

And nobody is getting calendars from me this year.

And what about the price of toys?

Electronic games — they can cost a fortune.

What about ordinary presents — bicycles! Almost a £100.

And I saw a doll's house at over £50. Imagine! A doll's house.

You can pay almost that for some of the dolls.

You can't get decent cheap things for the stocking.

I remember when children's annuals were only pennies — now they are pounds.

Yes — the price of toys frightens me.

The price of everything frightens me.

Even a box of chocolates — pounds and pounds they want for a decent box.

And three pounds for a small box of crackers.

It's frightening to think what the Christmas dinner is really going to cost.

It's not just the price of the turkey — it's all the trimmings.

Yes — Christmas is an expensive time.

No — I don't know how we can afford Christmas. It's too dear.

14   What Easter Means

What is Easter all about?
It's about the rebirth of nature.
Spring life coming from winter death.
Crocuses.
Snowdrops.
Daffodils.
Where does the cross of Christ fit in?
What is Easter all about?
It's about a spring holiday.
Hot cross buns.
Easter bonnets.
Easter eggs.
Easter brides.
Where does the cross of Christ fit in?
What is Easter all about?
It's about Lent — giving up things.
Special religious services.
Easter communion.
Good Friday.
What's good about the cross of Christ?
And where does the risen Jesus fit in today?

15   Testimony of a Non-Christian

My parents were faithful members of the Church and my
father was an elder. So I wasn't brought up a heathen. I
mean I did go to Sunday School and Bible Class and
eventually joined the Youth Fellowship. I was pretty
regular at church on Sundays although it didn't really

mean much to me. I suppose I did go just to please my parents and because most of my pals were in church.

As I say, it didn't mean much to me either then or now. Looking back I realise there were moments when I felt it ought to mean something. I remember I was once roped into going to an evangelical rally. You know, the Billy Graham sort of thing: slick, polished and all highly geared to create the maximum amount of emotion. I can't remember much of what the preacher said, but his appeal at the end really stuck in my mind. I really wanted to go forward; I even remember thinking of going round to see some of the counsellors after the meeting. Of course now I know it was all stage-managed with the tear-jerking 'Just as I am' and the highly charged emotional music. But at that moment I really wanted to give my life to Christ and make a fresh start. But I didn't go forward. It's funny how you want to do something yet you don't do it. I remember saying to myself that I should think it over first. So I just went home, and, of course, didn't think it over. I just didn't think about it at all.

It was from about that time I started to dodge church on occasional Sundays. Of course father and mother were often at me to join the Church and once the minister spoke to me about it. I just evaded them. I used to say I wanted to think it over; I discovered it was a good excuse because they said they respected me for it. The truth was I didn't do anything about the Christian faith or the Church. I found that I had more important things to think about. I was young and there were girls, parties, drinks and endless friends. By the time I was 20 I never thought of going to church.

I got married — in church of course — and set about carving a career for myself. I was a salesman and although I say it myself I was, and am, a good salesman. Sure it was hard work, a lot of pressure and a lot of travelling but the rewards were good. Sunday became the day for the golf course or a run in the car with my wife.

So that's it. I'm not a Christian, don't go to church. But I'm a success. Many envy me. I can earn anything from ten to twenty thousand a year. I've three credit cards in my wallet, my own Mercedes and my wife has a Mini. I've my own bungalow, holidays abroad twice a year — you name it and I've got it. Yes — I'm a success.

Now I know you are waiting for me to say 'but'. Well, I will admit that there are a few 'buts' in my life. I think everyone has a lot of 'buts' in their life. So I'm a success — but, yes I do sometimes wonder what it's all about. I work at full stretch and have an odd night out with the boys or a meal out with my wife. But is this really living? Yes, I wonder. At times I've got to try and convince myself that it really is. But I admit I'm not sure. It all seems to add up to a nice job, a nice wife, a nice house and it will all end up with a nice funeral.

But I don't really want to think about it. I just want to work and play. That's why, in my heart I have a secret dread of getting a coronary or a stroke; to be stuck in bed and to lie and think would drive me crazy. Maybe if I sat and really thought about it I would realise that in spite of my fine living I don't really have much of real life — whatever that is. Of course maybe everyone is like that, I don't know.

But I am haunted by the thought of what might have been. If I had gone forward that night at that rally what might I have done with my life? But I've made my life. As I say, I'm not a Christian but I am a success.

16   Last Will and Testament

What sort of heritage is being handed on? Is it something like this?

Herewith legal document duly signed and attested.

We, the older generation, hereby revoke all wills and testamental documents hitherto made by us.

We, the older generation, being of unsound mind and inflamed passions, hereby declare this to be our last will and testament.

We give and bequeath to the generations that follow us: the earth with its beauties and glories, and we leave anarchism; racialism; nationalism; communism; fascism; capitalism; militantism; materialism; paganism; agnosticism; atheism; pessimism; nihilism.

To the beloved children of our loins we bequeath the fearful toys of our hands: revolvers; rifles; bayonets; machine guns; flamethrowers; missiles; jackboots; atomic bombs; hydrogen bombs; neutron bombs.

We give and bequeath the sickness of sin that has corrupted our race.

And Jesus said: 'Peace I leave with you; my peace I give you. I do not give to you as the world gives. Do not let your hearts be troubled and do not be afraid... Do not let your hearts be troubled. Trust in God; trust in me... Take heart! I have overcome the world.'

17   Mayday

Mayday. Mayday. Mayday.
Planet out of control.
Have power but unable to regulate.
Compass erratic.
Directional instruments malfunctioning.
All readings false.
Destination unknown.

Mayday. Mayday. Mayday.
Planet out of control.
Mutiny on board.
King has been dethroned.
Commander's commandments disregarded.
Insurrection rampant.
Treason and sedition reign.
All laws ignored.
Planet out of control.

Mayday. Mayday. Mayday.

He came into the world.
And the world was made by him,
But the world knew him not.
He came unto his own
But His own received him not.
And they crucified him.
Mayday.

Warning.
Red alert. Red alert. Red alert.
King is returning.
His armies mobilising
Marshalling overwhelming forces

With infinitely more superior firepower.
King is planning to return.
Every knee will bow,
Every tongue confess
That he is Lord.
Red alert. Red alert. Red alert.

18   This is Living?

They tell me this is living.
To drink without thirst,
Feast without hunger,
And have sex without love.
To give way to animal passions
And live like a beast.

They tell me this is living.
To eat, drink and be happy
By fuddling the brain with alcohol,
Confusing the senses by drugs
And live by forgetting life
So that we can laugh without joy.

They tell me this is living.
Getting on in the world,
Accumulating wealth
And tasting the sweet nectar of success.

Living, they say, is
Having a big job,
Earning a big salary,
Boasting a big bankbook,
And living in a big house

While driving around in a big car
Earning a big reputation
As a big man.

They tell me this is living,
Forgetting to add that it will all end in
A big funeral.

II
ILLUSIONS OF LIFE

1   The Illusion of all Roads

Men today say there are many ways to God. Men say that all religions lead to God; that all religions are striving after the truth.

Jesus may have said: 'I am the way. No one comes to the Father but by me.'

But men say: 'At heart all religions are the same.'

But all religions include:

Monotheism — there is only one God.

Polytheism — there are many gods.

Pantheism — the world is god.

Atheism — there is no god.

How can these all be the same?

Think of Hinduism:

There the divine is plural and impersonal.

But in Islam, god is singular and personal.

While in Buddhism, god is neither personal nor creative.

How can these be the same?

In Buddhism there is no forgiveness.

In Christianity there is.

In Buddhism there is no supernatural aid.

In Christianity there is.

In Buddhism the goal of life is nirvana — that is extinction.

In Christianity the goal of life is being eternally with God in heaven.

Jesus said: 'I am the way, the truth, and the life. No one comes to the Father but by me.'

2   The Illusion of Education

Apparently we live in a sophisticated and enlightened age. Today we consider ourselves to have progressed in literacy and knowledge from the ignorance of a few centuries ago.

Yet we live in an age when universities are having to run remedial classes in reading and composition for students.

In the past children's books were of a high literary standard with such authors as R L Stevenson and Lewis Carroll writing lengthy books full of content.

Today comic and television dominate.

In the past children in Scotland had to master the Shorter Catechism and so had a good knowledge of what the Christian faith taught.

It is not cynical to suggest that most adult members of the churches today would find it hard to answer such catechism questions as:

What is sin?
What is effectual calling?
Justification?
Adoption?
Sanctification?
The duty God requires of man?

A study of the curricula of the early non-conformist schools in England in the late 17th century indicates the scope of study.

Logic.
Metaphysics.
Philosophy.
Divinity.
Anatomy.
Mechanics.
Jewish antiquities.

Mythology.

Hieroglyphics.

Now most are interested in entertainment rather than instruction; in enjoying themselves rather than in widening the horizons of their knowledge.

Apparently we live in a sophisticated and enlightened age. Today we consider ourselves to have progressed in literacy and knowledge from the ignorance of a few centuries ago.

3   The Illusion of Advertisements

Adverts concentrate on trying to implant an 'urge to buy' rather than giving information.

They focus almost solely on the psychological instincts within us, to influence and manipulate our choice.

Adverts don't sell goods — they sell dreams.

Lipsticks and beauty creams are not advertised as chemical concoctions but as something to give a dream of beauty, sexual fulfilment and poise.

Men's toiletries are presented as a dream fulfilment of masculine attractiveness and sexual prowess.

Alcohol is presented as fulfilling the dream of strength, social acceptance and comradeship.

Adverts are not in the business of promoting goods — they are in the business of selling dreams and wish fulfilments.

Adverts appeal to maternal instincts.

'Good mothers' always use 'this' soap powder, feed their family with 'that' particular foodstuff, or buy 'this' brand for their homes.

You know the little boy with his shorts caked in mud whose mother simply smiles and welcomes the dirty shorts as an opportunity to use her favourite soap powder.

Adverts appeal to sex.

Women, scantily dressed and glamorous, are used to sell an astonishing range of goods.

Cars and chocolates are presented on television with husky 'sexy' voices and soft music in glamorous settings.

Certain aftershave lotions and pipe tobaccos are shown as things that, if a man uses them, will make women throw themselves at his feet.

Adverts appeal to envy.

A great number of adverts play upon envy, greed and selfishness, implying that you deserve to spoil yourself.

After all, if some soap is good enough for film stars, is it not good enough for you?

If some film star likes a certain brand of coffee then you can be as good as him by drinking the same coffee.

Adverts appeal to science.

Toothpastes are presented as containing miracle ingredients which are meaningless to the consumer.

We are told that some soap powders wash 'biologically' — whatever this means!

Others wash whiter than white — whatever that means!

Adverts appeal to happiness.

Adverts present a world where goods equal happiness.

A chocolate bar leads to paradise!

Adverts encourage us on the pathway of possessions.

Yet Jesus asserted: 'A man's life does not consist in the abundance of his possessions.' (Luke 12:15)

4   The Illusion of Television

There can be little doubt that television is a dominant factor in our society. People watch, on average, three hours a day. Most news is absorbed from the television rather than newspapers. Television is presented as a window on the world and most people unthinkingly accept it as such.

After all, we can see things exactly as they happen, and we trust our own eyes.

What is often forgotten is that television is a window that a man controls.

We see what a camera is pointed at, and that camera is directed by a man.

We see what we are intended to see.

There is the danger that television reduces everything to one level.

Everything is presented as a show.

Even the news, current affairs and educational programmes must be entertaining.

The Miss World contest is treated as almost as important as a general election.

The Eurovision Song Contest is treated as of breathless importance.

Yet a Ministerial broadcast is regarded as a boring interruption of the real programmes.

What effect does this have on us?

What is the effect of seeing starving victims or the casualties of an earthquake?

Our emotional response is dulled — for what can we do?

Such tragedy is quickly forgotten as our attention is diverted to sport or comedy.

We think we are in touch with reality — but are we?

Someone has said: 'The proddings of an Orwell only break the rhythm of our ruminating jaws as, with eyes intent on the fatal screen, we sink ever further from reality.'

5   The Illusion of Progress

Of course there has been progress. There has been progress in medicine; in technology; in travel; in knowledge about the world we live in.

But has man progressed?

Of course we have progressed technologically.

But is it all for the good?

Robots replace men.

Men now serve machines instead of machines serving men.

The microchip has made men redundant.

Of course we have progressed in education.

But is it all for the good?

Specialisation has created a generation that knows more and more about less and less.

Have we progressed in behaviour?

There is moral permissiveness.

And anarchy in the classroom.

Violence on the street.

And we kill helpless children before they are born.

Have we progressed in knowledge and ability?

Yes — just think — we have moved from

Fists to clubs.

Clubs to spears.

Spears to bow and arrows.
Bow and arrows to crossbows.
Crossbows to guns.
Guns to cannons.
Cannons to bombs.
Bombs to rockets.
Rockets to atom bombs.
Atom to hydrogen bombs.
And hydrogen to neutron bombs.
Now we can blow up the world.
Boy! Have we progressed!

NB: Lines in italics should be spoken by a separate voice.

6 Illusions about Faith

Faith is the basis of the Christian life. And Christian faith is grounded in the sure word of God. But people have many strange ideas about faith. They say:

Faith is believing what you know is not true.
It's a leap in the dark.
It's believing what you can't prove.
Faith is wishful thinking.
It's a belief in something for which there is no evidence.
Faith tramples underfoot all reason, sense and understanding.
It's an illogical belief in the occurrence of the improbable.
Faith is mere pious conviction.
A blind and empty hope.
Faith is believing what you know isn't true.
Faith is an escape from reality.

Faith is believing unbelievable things.
Impossible things.
Faith is gullible.

7   The Illusion of Religion

To have illusions about God and his revealed Gospel is the
most devastating of all illusions. Yet we are encircled by
the illusions of false prophets offering a false peace
through false ceremonies.

There are false prophets.
They say that all roads lead to God and that all religions
are different expressions of 'the truth'.
They teach that we can find acceptance with God by
doing good.
Often false prophets give a reduction of biblical truth.
And as G K Chesterton once remarked: 'Half truths,
like half bricks, often do the most damage.'
Then there is a false peace
God said: 'They dress the wound of my people as
though it were not serious. "Peace, peace," they say,
when there is no peace.' (Jer. 6:14).
And people are always ready for such comforting illusions.
God wants us to have peace but it will not be found by
listening to the siren voices of the false prophets.
They think that God does not really care about our little
sins.
That religion is all right in small doses.
That there is really no hell to worry about.
Then there are false ceremonies.
Many seem to think that certain ceremonies keep them
all right with God.

Many observe Christian ceremonies and rituals and feel that this is to their credit.

Think of those who want their baby 'done' — that is baptised.

Many join the Church — to be married. It is much nicer than a registry office wedding.

But it is also possible to attend church twice every Sunday; to have regular Bible reading and personal devotions and to think that by such activity we keep in with God.

Personal attempts at rightness with God can become false piety.

God denounces hollow ritualism.

What pleases God is only the heart pierced by his word and vitalised by his spirit.

8   The Illusion of Reality

It is widely felt that with the advent of modern means of communication we are more knowledgeable about the reality of the world and life than ever before. But are we? Is not the danger that we are taking the image for the reality?

A sociologist tells of a woman admiring a baby and being told: 'That's nothing, you should see his photo.'

Aldous Huxley told the story of seeing a couple sitting in their car at the Grand Canyon. At the top of this great wonder of nature they were sitting looking through a hand-viewer at slides of the Grand Canyon!

In a radio lecture, Professor Aaron Scharf reported that at an exhibition of Gauguin in Chicago many complained that the reproductions on sale were actually better than the original paintings!

Even when we are watching newsreels and documentaries it is difficult to know when reality ends and the show begins. Often we cannot tell how often it has been rehearsed and staged.

A few years ago a newspaper reported an army commander in Belfast complaining that after his troops went into a difficult and hostile street, the television cameras arrived and asked him to send them in again so that they could film it.

David Wolper, Hollywood's king of TV documentaries, recently claimed that he was now making his own old newsreels.

We cannot tell how often a scene·has been rehearsed and staged — even news items.

Malcolm Muggeridge tells how, when he went to do an outside broadcast with colour cameras, there was a man with the team carrying a roll on his shoulder. When Muggeridge inquired what the roll of material was he was informed that it was plastic grass — the grass they were going to film was not green enough!

Again Muggeridge tells of a man jumping over the Berlin Wall at a quiet spot. The television cameras happened to be there — and the man had to jump three times before they got it right!

So what is reality?

9   The Illusion of Self

Men regard themselves as highly developed animals.
Evolutionary mutants.
Scientifically sophisticated.
Men think they can do all things.
Achieve all things.

Dominate all things.
Men think they can rule the world and suit themselves.
They think they know where they are going.
They think education can solve everything.
Men don't think they need God.
That they are not bad.
That they are decent.
That they are good.
Men don't think they need salvation.
Men don't think they are lost.
Men don't think they are sinners.·
They think, that if there is a God, he should be proud of them.
Men think they are as gods.
And the first lie was: disobey God and you shall be like God.

10   An Illusion of Belief

I believe in God the Father Almighty, maker of heaven and earth;
And in Jesus Christ his only son our Lord
Who was conceived by the Holy Ghost,
Born of the Virgin Mary,
Suffered under Pontius Pilate,
Was crucified, dead and buried;
He descended into hell,
The third day he rose again from the dead,
He ascended into heaven
And sitteth on the right hand of God the Father Almighty;
From thence he shall come to judge the quick and the dead.

I believe in the Holy Ghost,
The Holy Catholic Church;
The communion of saints;
The resurrection of the body;
And the life everlasting.

Yes. I believe.
    Yes. I believe.
    I believe in God the Father Almighty.
    I believe — yes, I believe in God, definitely.
    Maker of heaven and earth.
    Ah well — yes — I'm not sure about that; after all there's Darwin and all the latest scientific theories: Big Bang theory and Steady State theory and the Continuous Creation theory. I'm not sure about God being...
    And in Jesus Christ, his only son, our Lord.
    I believe — oh yes, I believe in Jesus. I'm not sure about 'only Son', what it means, but...
    Who was conceived by the Holy Ghost, born of the Virgin Mary.
    There you are again — born of a virgin. I mean... Well, I don't know.
    Suffered under Pontius Pilate, was crucified, dead and buried.
    Yes, oh yes, I believe that.
    He descended into hell.
    Well — yes — oh, I don't know. What does it mean?
    The third day he rose again from the dead.
    Ah well — yes — I don't know. What really happened anyway — empty tomb — no, I don't know.
    He ascended into heaven.
    This really has problems. In this space age there is neither up nor down. I don't know whether I believe that or not.
    And sitteth on the right hand of God, the Father Almighty.
    I don't know. I mean is heaven a place where Jesus can actually sit down? Is it a place at all — I — no, I'm sorry I don't know.

From thence he shall come to judge the quick and the dead.

No. Judgment is not something we talk about nowadays. I don't know if I believe it.

I believe in the Holy Ghost.

Oh yes, I believe in some sort of force or something to make us good — but — no, I'm not sure what I believe about that.

The Holy Catholic Church.

Yes, oh yes, I believe in the Church — well my church anyway.

The communion of saints.

Well — yes — well, some saints anyway. Yes.

The forgiveness of sins.

I suppose I do — though sins seems such an old-fashioned word.

The resurrection of the body.

I'm going to be cremated so I'm not sure we can talk about resurrection of the body. It's — oh I don't know.

And the life everlasting.

Heaven and all that sort of thing — no — I just don't know.

I believe.

I don't know.

I believe.

I'm not sure what I believe.

I believe.

I've never thought out what I believe. I've never really thought of it.

11   Illusions about the Church

What is the Church?

It is the building up the road.
Yes — old buildings with stained glass windows.
It can be new buildings — with stained glass windows.
Usually they are big empty barns.
Monuments to irrelevancy.
The Church — it's lots of denominations.
There is the Church of Scotland.
The Church of England.
The Roman Catholic Church.
The Methodist Church.
The Baptist Church.
And lots of bits and pieces.
It is big bureaucracies, institutions run by ministers and
priests.
And bishops, deacons, archbishops and canons.
Yes — and curates, elders and pastors.
The church is a place to get babies christened.
To get married.
And buried.
It is a place for a good sing.
To send the kids to Sunday School.
For meeting people.
But it is a place where they are always looking for
money.
Jumble sales.
Sales of work.
Coffee mornings.
It's a sort of holy huddle,
For people who are out of touch with real life.
For folk who want to live in the past.
The church is a sort of religious social club.
For the old and the young.
It is a place for Christmas, Easter and Harvest.
A place for pleasing God by going — two or three times a
year.

12   Testimony of Herod

I am Herod the Great, King of Judea. Yes, I know how
people remember me. I was the bloodthirsty King who
ordered the massacre of the innocents at Bethlehem. But
do you want to hear my side of the story? Let me tell you it.

I was King. And it is not easy being a king. You have
got to be alert all the time and ever aware of all politics,
plotting and scheming. Look at my problems with Rome.
You know I supported Mark Anthony and then, when he
was defeated, it took all my skill and ability to become an
ally of Octavius. I had to remain friends with Rome. So I
had theatres built and organised games there.

But the Jews do not like such things. I had to keep in
with them also. You've no idea the number of people
you've got to please when you're a king. So I rebuilt the
temple in Jerusalem. At least that earned me some credit
with the priests and religious authorities. And yet all the
time I was surrounded by enemies. There were endless
plots against me, even in my own household. I had to have
Alexander and Aristobulus executed. I know they were
my own sons, but I had my suspicions about them — they
wanted my throne. I even had to dispose of my wife
Mariamne. There was no end to the plots.

But you want to hear about this affair at Bethlehem. It
came about with an unexpected visit from some princes
from the East; Persia I think. Maybe they were not
princes, I don't know. Wise men, Magi, call them what
you will. Anyway, they came with shocking news. Here
was I, struggling to hold on to my throne — I knew there
were always plots going on — and then along come these
travellers. They had tales about a new-born king in Israel
and raved about signs in the heavens and stars and omens.
They wanted to know where the new king had been born.

So I sent for my tame priests and they mumbled and

talked until eventually they said the Scriptures foretold a king being born in Bethlehem. Of course they believe that sort of thing. It's their job I suppose. A new king! Of course I was angry at the idea. I was King. No one was going to take away my throne from me. But I managed to control my anger; I am good at that.

So I sent these strange travellers to Bethlehem to do the finding out for me. After all, if I had sent my troops these Jews would probably have hidden the baby king. But I told the travellers — and this was clever I think — to come back and let me know where I could find the new king so that I could go and worship him. Yes, I was going to worship him all right.

And they never came back. No — they didn't come back. Those vile Persians deceived me. They cheated me — King Herod, friend of Rome! If only I could get my hands on them. I would teach them a lesson or two. Princes or not they would never see their homes again. No one deceives Herod the Great!

So what was I to do? Sit back and wait for the rebellion? I did the only thing I could do. I made sure the new-born king would not live long enough to start a revolution against me. In a way I stopped a civil war before it got started; and that marks me out as a man of vision, a clever king. It wasn't just politics, it was statesmanship; I ended a civil war before it started.

That is why I ordered that all male children born in Bethlehem around that time should be put to the sword. Just to be on the safe side I made the order apply to all boys under two years of age. It was a quick and sensible decision. I was not going to wait until there was a bloodbath. I was King and was going to remain King.

God? Did you say God? Did I hear someone say God? What has God got to do with it? I can do what I like. I am King. Anyway it was a political decision. What has God got to do with politics?

13   Testimony of Caiaphas

I am Caiaphas, High Priest of Israel. I was appointed to this office by Valerius Gratus, the immediate predecessor of Pontius Pilate. Yesterday I played a large part in the death of this man Jesus. I am not ashamed of that; I have no need to justify myself. I was the High Priest. And what was he — a carpenter from Nazareth! So I ask you — who is right? A high priest or a carpenter who could work tricks and dazzle the people with his fancy words?

I know he claimed to be more than a prophet; claimed to be equal with God. I didn't need to hear him, examine the evidence or anything like that. I just knew he was a fake. Anyway I was the High Priest and who do you think God would speak through: me or a nonentity from Nazareth? Who ever heard of anything or anyone good coming from Nazareth? The people should have listened to me, I was their High Priest. But it just shows how gullible and stupid the people are. They followed this man in droves.

It was a difficult time. But true leadership is seeing what is happening and knowing what to do about it. So I provided leadership. The important thing was not to let things get out of hand, and make sure that we kept Rome happy. Yes, we had to obey Rome and keep the peace.

So I knew we had to get rid of this Jesus. Get rid of him quickly and quietly. I laid my plans carefully. We were fortunate in getting a traitor from among his own followers. Judas was worth more than the 30 pieces of silver he cost us. So we got him, this so-called prophet from Nazareth. Now I admit I wanted him killed. It was the only solution to the problem. Sometimes it is necessary that one man should die rather than the whole nation. He had to die.

I know that some of my brethren were unhappy about

the means I had to use. Maybe the Sanhedrin council had some slight illegal technicalities. I know it had not been duly constituted and it should not have met at night, and maybe we did not have a quorum but these are trivial matters. The important thing was to get rid of Jesus of Galilee. Sometimes it is necessary to ignore the law to uphold the law. Anyway I was the High Priest and knew what had to be done.

Pilate, of course, gave me some cause for alarm. He wanted to know what Jesus had done! However I did not get where I am today without knowing how to manipulate people like Pilate. I just needed to whisper 'Rome' in his ear and he was quivering with fear.

Although I say it myself it was a satisfactory job well done. Yesterday we got rid of Jesus once and for all. Now, no one will ever hear of him again. The few followers he had are already in hiding. They are just nobodies and nothings while I remain High Priest.

Now you must excuse me, I have my evening prayers to attend.

14   The Mad Merchant

He was a merchant,
A merchant such as no one had ever seen before,
Wheeling his wares around the world
And offering his goods to all people
From his bounteous bargain bazaar.
With sweet-sounding words and silver tongue
He promised unrepeatable offers with
Unbreakable guarantees.
But he was only a merchant,
A mad merchant

A silly salesman who offered all he had
Freely and for nothing.
But he had only things that few could want:
Strange commodities like
Forgiveness. Salvation. Redemption.
And unheard-of products like
Peace. Love. Joy. Contentment.
Such were the offers of the merchant.
The mad merchant,
Who offered all things
Without money and without price.
Few were fooled,
We did not buy.
But we made him pay dearly for what he offered.
We crucified him.

III
THE SOURCE OF LIFE

1   The Threefold Word

How do we know God? How can we know anything about an infinite and eternal God — for we are finite, children of time? We only know because God has revealed himself. God has spoken. But how has he spoken to us?

He speaks to us in creation.
He speaks to us in Scripture.
He speaks to us in Christ.
God speaks to us through his word in creation.
The heavens declare the glory of God.
The earth is full of his handiwork.
In creation we see: order.
                   design.
                   beauty.
                   simplicity.
                   harmony.
And thus we know that God is a god of order, beauty and harmony.
God speaks to us through his word in Scripture.
There he tells of the root dilemma of man, our dilemma of sin.
And there he tells us the glorious plan of salvation.
Of his righteousness.
His law.
His justice.
His holiness.
His love.
His goodness.
His grace.
His mercy.

65

His forgiveness.
His offer of eternal life in Christ.
And thus we know something of the character and
    standards of the God who is there.
God speaks to us through the living word: Jesus Christ
    who is full of grace and truth.
For in Jesus we see the fulfilment of the law of God.
In him we see the holiness of God.
In him we see the love of God.
In him we have the forgiveness of God.
For in him dwells the fulness of God.
So God is not an unknown God.
We know God.
Because God has revealed himself to us.
He spoke, and all things were.
He speaks in his written word: the Bible.
He speaks in his living word: the Incarnate Christ.

2   The Sovereignty of God

So often we have an impoverished idea of God. Our God
    is too small.
What is our picture of God?
Often we imagine him as — a benign old man.
A sort of heavenly Santa Claus.
A cosmic message boy — to get things done.
A divine doctor — to summon in times of trouble.
A celestial policeman — to punish others who do wrong.
Often we imagine that God is a passive spectator watching
    a world that has gone out of control.
Or just someone who lived long, long ago.
But how does God reveal himself? Listen to what he says:
I am the Creator — and there is none beside me.

I am from everlasting to everlasting.
Mine is the greatness.
The power.
The glory.
The majesty.
The splendour.
Everything in heaven and earth is mine.
I am the ruler of all things.
I am enthroned above the earth.
I am all powerful.
All knowing.
All seeing.
I am sovereign over all things.
To whom will you compare me? Or who is my equal?
I am the sovereign God.

3   The Promises of God

God makes many promises. Among these promises are:

God promises us peace.
  'I will keep in perfect peace, him whose mind is steadfast and because he trusts in me.' (*Cf* Isa 26:3)

God promises us his presence.
  'As I was with Moses, so I will be with you; I will never leave you or forsake you.' (Josh 1:5)

God promises us his provision.
  'He will sustain you; he will never let the righteous fall.' (Ps 55:22)

God promises us deliverance in trouble.
  'He will deliver the needy who cry out, the afflicted who have no one to help.' (Ps 72:12)

God promises us guidance.

'In all your ways acknowledge him, and he will make your paths straight.' (Prov 3:6)

God promises his sufficiency in our weakness.

'My grace is sufficient for you, for my power is made perfect in weakness.' (2 Cor 12:9)

God promises us mercy.

'Let the wicked forsake his way...let him turn to the Lord, and he will have mercy on him...for he will freely pardon.' (Isa 55:7)

God promises us everlasting life.

'I am the resurrection and the life. He who believes in me will live, even though he dies.' (John 11:25)

God promises us an eternal inheritance.

'Through the resurrection of Jesus Christ you have an inheritance that can never perish, spoil or fade — kept in heaven for you by God's power.' (*Cf* 1 Peter 1:4-5)

4   The Gospel is

The Gospel is — that all have sinned and fall short of the glory of God.
This means I have sinned.
It means you have sinned.
The Gospel is — that all are guilty before a holy and just God.
This means I am guilty.
This means you are guilty.
The Gospel is — God so loved the world that he sent Jesus.

This means God loves me and sent Jesus for me.
This means God loves you and sent Jesus for you.
The Gospel is — Jesus died for the sins of the world.
This means Jesus died for me.
This means Jesus died for you.
The Gospel is — that Jesus died — but rose again and so
   he comes with the offer of salvation, to the world.
This means he comes to me.
This means he comes to you.
I have turned to him.
Will you?
I admit I am a sinner.
Will you?
I have taken Christ to be my Saviour.
Will you?

5   God will come

In the beginning God created the heavens and the earth
and saw that it was very good. He created man in his own
image, making him a little lower than the angels,
crowning him with glory and honour, and making him
Lord of Creation.

But man rebelled against God and sin entered. Instead
of being free servants of God, man by rebelling became
the slave of sin, the servant of Satan, and a citizen of the
kingdom of darkness. With sin, a great barrier came
between God and man, a barrier no man could break
down.

But, from the time Adam sinned, God promised
deliverance. He promised One who would break down the
barrier between God and man. Listen to the promises of
God concerning the one whom he would send.

'And the Lord God said unto the serpent, I will put enmity between thee and the woman, and between thy seed and her seed; it shall bruise thy head, and thou shalt bruise his heel.' (Gen 3:15 AV)

'Behold, a virgin shall conceive, and bear a son, and shall call his name Immanuel' — which is God with us (Isa 7:14 AV)

'And his name shall be called Wonderful, Counsellor, The mighty God, The everlasting Father, The Prince of Peace. Of the increase of his government and peace there shall be no end.' (Isa 9:6-7 AV)

'For thus saith the Lord God: Behold I, even I, will both search for my sheep, and seek them out. As a shepherd seeketh out his flock in the day...that [they] are scattered; so will I seek out my sheep, and will deliver them...in the cloudy and dark day.' (*Cf* Ezek 34:11-12 AV)

'They shall cry unto the Lord because of the oppressors, and he shall send them a saviour, and a great one, and he shall deliver them.' (Isa 19:20 AV)

'And the glory of the Lord shall be revealed, and all flesh shall see it together: for the mouth of the Lord hath spoken it.' (Isa 40:5 AV)

'Behold the Lord God will come with a strong hand, and his arm shall rule for him...he shall feed his flock like a shepherd: he shall gather the lambs with his arm, and carry them in his bosom, and shall gently lead those that are with young.' (Isa 40:10-11 AV)

'And there shall come forth a rod out of the stem of Jesse, and a Branch shall grow out of his roots: and the spirit of the Lord shall rest upon him.' (Isa 11:1 AV)

'The kings of Tarshish and of the isles shall bring presents...Yea, all kings shall fall down before him; all nations shall serve him. He shall spare the poor and needy, and shall save the souls of the needy.' (Ps 72:10-12 AV)

'But thou, Bethlehem...though thou be little among the thousands of Judah, yet out of thee shall he come forth

unto me that is to be ruler in Israel; whose goings forth
have been...from everlasting.' (Mic 5:2 AV)

6   Memo to Gabriel — First Christmas

The Prince of Glory will descend to the fallen planet earth.
He will leave his glory behind and take his place among
men as a man. The following arrangements must be made
for this reclamation of the fallen planet.

1 Zechariah, Priest of the Temple, must be informed that
   his wife, Elizabeth, will bear a son whose name will be
   John. This child will have the spirit and power of Elijah
   and will make ready, in the fulness of time, the way of
   the Lord.
2 Angel must inform Mary, virgin of Nazareth, engaged
   to Joseph the Carpenter, that she will be the mother of
   the child Prince.
3 To avoid problems for the proposed marriage between
   Joseph and Mary, an angel must be despatched to
   advise Joseph of the full facts of Mary's pregnancy.
   Joseph must be instructed to call the child Jesus.
4 Arrangements must be made to ensure that a bright
   star is in the required position, at the correct time, over
   Persia. This star will be used to guide the men of
   wisdom from the East to Bethlehem where the Prince
   will become a baby.
5 An angel must be authorised to inform the shepherds
   near Bethlehem when the Prince becomes a baby and
   makes his appearance on earth.
6 Immediately following the announcement to the shepherds a great company of Angelic Host must be
   assembled above the plains of Bethlehem. They
   sing a joyous anthem to the glory of God.

7 When the men of wisdom from the East visit the child prince they must be warned not to inform Herod where the child is staying. The enemy will attempt to use Herod to kill the young prince.

8 On the departure of the men of wisdom from the East, Joseph must be warned that the child is in great danger. He should be instructed to go, with Mary and child, into Egypt. They will be informed when to return.

7 What Christmas Really Costs

Christmas is an expensive time for us isn't it? But what was the cost of Christmas for Jesus? What did it cost him? 'He came unto his own, and his own received him not.' (John 1:11 AV)

'Christ Jesus: Who, being in very nature God, did not consider equality with God something to be grasped, but made himself nothing, taking the very nature of a servant, being made in human likeness.' (Phil 2:6-7)

> Unresisting he renounced,
> Like borrowed things
> Omnipotence and the power to work miracles;
> Now he was mortal like ourselves. (Boris Pasternak)

> Lo! within a manager lies
> He who built the starry skies,
> He who throned in height sublime,
> Sits amid the cherubim. (Edward Carswell)

> He came down to earth from heaven
> Who is God and Lord of all,
> And his shelter was a stable,
> And his cradle was a stall.
> With the poor and mean and lowly
> Lived on earth our Saviour holy.
>   (Cecil Frances Alexander)

'He came — and he came to die.'

'Jesus, the author and perfector of our faith, who for the joy set before him endured the cross.' (Heb 12:2)

'He was despised and rejected by men, a man of sorrows, and familiar with suffering. Like one from whom men hide their faces he was despised, and we esteemed him not.' (Isa 53:3)

> He left his Father's throne above,
> So free, so infinite his grace,
> Emptied himself of all but love,
> And bled for Adam's helpless race. (Charles Wesley)

'He was pierced for our transgressions, he was crushed for our iniquities; the punishment that brought us peace was upon him, and by his wounds we are healed.' (Isa 53:5)

> See! from his head, his hands, his feet,
> Sorrow and love flow mingled down;
> Did e'er such love and sorrow meet,
> Or thorns compose so rich a crown? (Isaac Watts)

'He was oppressed and afflicted, yet he did not open his mouth.' (Isa 53:7)

'He was cut off from the land of the living; for the transgression of my people he was stricken.' (Isa 53:8)

'He came unto his own, and his own received him not.' (John 1:11 AV)

And they crucified him.

8   Who is Jesus?

Who is Jesus?
Wonderful Counsellor.
The mighty God.

The everlasting Father.
The Prince of Peace.
Jesus is the Second Person of the Trinity.
He is God.
Creator.
Through him all things were made.
He is Lawgiver.
The Light of the world.
Alpha and Omega.
First and Last.
Jesus is the one who came into the world — from heaven.
As suffering servant.
Prophet.
Priest.
King.
Redeemer.
Mediator.
Saviour.
Lamb of God.
The Lamb slain from the foundation of the world.
The Christ of God.
Son of man.
Son of God.
Jesus is, to the Christian today,
Saviour.
Lord.
Interceder.
Bridegroom.
Elder brother.
King.
Jesus is the one who will return.
As conquering King.
Before whom every knee will bow.
And every tongue confess.
Jesus Christ is Lord.
Jesus will be the Lamb who will reign.

Worthy is the Lamb who was slain, to receive power and
wealth and wisdom and strength and honour and glory
and praise. To him who sits upon the throne and to the
Lamb be praise and honour and glory and power, for
ever and ever.

9 Witnesses to Jesus' Identity

Who is Jesus?

Nicodemus said: 'You are a teacher who has come from
God.' (John 3:2)

The temple guards sent to arrest him said: 'No-one ever
spoke the way this man does.' (John 7:46)

A soldier at the cross said: 'Surely this was a righteous
man.' (Luke 23:47)

Andrew said: 'We have found the Messiah.' (John 1:41)

Samaritans said: 'This man really is the Saviour of the
world.' (John 4:42)

Nathaniel said: 'You are the Son of God; you are the
King of Israel.' (John 1:49)

During his ministry Peter declared: 'You are the
Christ, the Son of the living God.' (Matt 16:16)

Martha said: 'I believe that you are the Christ, the Son
of God.' (John 11:27)

Thomas said: 'My Lord and my God!' (John 20:28)

John wrote: 'The Word became flesh (John 1:14). And
the Word was God.' (John 1:1)

Paul said: 'There is one God and one mediator between
God and men, the man Christ Jesus.' (1 Tim 2:5)

'For in Christ all the fulness of the Deity lives in bodily
form.' (Col 2:9)

'For by him all things were created.' (Col 1:16)

At the outset of his ministry John the Baptist declared:
'Look, the Lamb of God.' (John 1:29)

Scripture tells us: 'The Lamb will overcome ... because ... he is Lord of lords and King of kings.' (Rev 17:14)

The writer of Hebrews said: 'Jesus Christ is the same yesterday and today and for ever.' (Heb 13:8)

Who do you think he is?

10   A Letter from John

John, son of Zebedee, to his brother James, much beloved.

I pray that mother and father are well. Give them my love and tell them my prayers are with them. I hope the family fishing business is prospering, even without me, the angry dreamer as I have been called.

I know many look upon me as a disappointment to the family but there is so much happening and I have had to find out for myself. I am still with the Baptist, but this letter is to say that I may be moving on to find out about another. James, believe me, the Baptist is a prophet of the High, Eternal One. I am daily more convinced of this. He is a remarkable man. Everyone, from the towns, villages and even from Jerusalem, is coming to the Jordan to hear John preach and to be baptised. No one can speak with the strength and conviction of John the Baptist unless they were of God.

You should come and hear him. It would warm your heart to hear how he condemns and fearlessly denounces the cold religious leaders from Jerusalem. You know how they love to complicate everything and make the Law of Moses an impossible burden. John is so simple. Some tax-collectors came to be baptised. They asked what they should do to please God. Can you imagine how the

Pharisees would answer that question? The Baptist simply said, 'Don't collect any more than you are required to.' In a word, he was telling them to be honest — and isn't that what God wants? Another day some soldiers asked the same question. John told them, 'Don't exhort money and don't accuse people falsely — be content with your pay.' It is only now I am beginning to see what God requires of us — repentance and faithfulness.

Sometimes I fear for John's life. But there are a number of us here who will fight to the death for this prophet and the people will be on our side.

But — and this is the purpose of this letter — maybe more than a prophet has come. John has always said that he is but the herald proclaiming the coming of the Kingdom. If the Kingdom is coming does that not mean the King is coming? Or is he here? Let me tell you what has happened to make me think on these lines.

One day, as always, there were long queues of people waiting to be baptised by John. Then, when one person reached John there was a long delay. I went forward to see what was happening and it was a strange sight. John was standing in the water looking at this man and the man was standing looking at John. They were staring deeply into each other's eyes without speaking. I think they were strangers, but it was as if they knew one another in a deep way, maybe beyond human knowledge. I don't know. Then a remarkable thing happened. John shook his head slowly as if waking from a dream and said, and I could hear pain and wonder in his voice: 'I need to be baptised of you and do you come to me?' Then this man replied quietly: 'Let it be so now; it is proper for us to do this to fulfill all righteousness.'

So John baptised this man. Now, what happened next I am not sure. It seemed as if the heavens were opened — there was light such as I have never seen before. Then something like a dove came down to hover over the man's head and there was a sound like a voice from heaven. I know there were words but I could not tell what they said. One day the man will tell us, I know.

Later John would not talk about this experience or what happened. But it has got us all talking. All we learned was that the man was named Jesus and is a carpenter from Nazareth. Later we saw him again. This time John pointed to him and said: 'Look, the Lamb of God who takes away the sin of the world.' It was a strange thing to say but he would not tell us any more. But he kept talking about the one who was coming who would increase while he, John, decreased. It was all so strange and Andrew and I talked about it late into the night..

The following day Andrew and I were walking along the Jordan with the Baptist when he suddenly pointed: 'Look, the Lamb of God.' We looked and saw this Jesus. Now Andrew and I have decided to go and see Jesus. We are not sure where he is staying at the moment but we feel we must find him. Is he the promised one of whom John and the other prophets spoke? What does it mean: 'a lamb'? John says little but I know he will be in favour of us finding out for ourselves. So we are going to this Jesus. We must find out the truth.

James, I am not mad. You, as my brother, know that. But I admit I am wondering if this Jesus could be the King. Maybe I am being foolish. Can a carpenter be a king? Is God sending a lamb rather than a deliverer? My mind is in a whirl and my thoughts torturous. But I want to find out about this Jesus for myself.

I will write to you later and let you know what I have learned about this Jesus whom John says is the Lamb of God.

Your loving brother,

John

11   Things Jesus did

Jesus taught:
Jesus taught of our need of salvation, that we are guilty
   before God.
Jesus taught us the way to God.
He taught us that he is the way.
And he taught us how to live.
And how to pray.
He taught that he was the Son of God.
That he must die to pay the price of sin.
And that he would rise again.
He taught that he would come back.
Jesus performed miracles.
He healed countless people.
He walked on water.
He fed over 5000 with five rolls and two fish.
He raised the dead.
He raised Jairus' daughter.
And the son of a widow in Nain.
And Lazarus.
Jesus died.
And rose again.
He ascended into heaven.
He sits at God the Father's right hand.
From where he will come to judge the living and the dead.
And that means that it is not just something that
   happened long ago.
He is alive — now.

12   What Jesus was like

We do not know how tall he was, the colour of his hair or

eyes, or what he looked like. But these things do not matter. What we know is this:

He was full of compassion.
Acquainted with grief.
No one spoke like him.
He was a brilliant debater.
And had a dominant personality.
He was authoritative.
Fearless.
Holy.
He was compassionate.
Meek.
Lowly.
Humble.
Gentle.
Kind.
Considerate.
Thoughtful.
Merciful.
Tolerant.
He was compassionate.
But he could also be righteously angry.
Consumed with a holy jealousy.
Zealous for God.
Uncompromising.
Intolerant of sin and evil.
He was compassionate. Full of grace and truth.
The perfect reflection of the character of God.
Totally good.
Totally committed.
Totally obedient.
Totally holy.
Totally loving and compassionate.

13 Supposing Jesus had never Lived

Christ came to save. He came unto his own, and his own received him not. Suppose that there had never been a Christmas. Suppose it was always winter and never Christmas. It would mean that Jesus had not come. Supposing Jesus had never lived.

Then there would have been no Church.
No disciples.
No New Testament.
No Christmas.
No Easter.
No crosses.
There would have been no saints, like Francis of Assissi.
No Martin Luther.
No John Wesley.
No missionaries.
No David Livingstone.
No Gladys Aylward.
No Martin Luther King.
No Corrie Ten Boom.
No C S Lewis.
No civil rights.
No Christian Aid.
No Tear Fund.
No Bible Societies.
No prison reform.
No social reform.
No Red Cross.
No hospitals.
No Christian compassion.
No Salvation Army.
If Jesus never lived there would be:

No Church.
No hymns to sing.
No children's choruses.
No Sunday Schools.
No Bible classes.
No Youth Fellowships.
No ministers.
No eventide homes.
No hope.
No peace.
No Christian love.
No forgiveness.
No power to love.
If Jesus had not come at Christmas, none of us would be here just now.
But Jesus came.
He was in the world, and though the world was made through him, the world did not recognise him. He came to that which was his own, but his own did not receive him.
Yet to all who received him, to those who believed in his name, he gave the right to become children of God.

14   A Letter to Emmaus

Jerusalem

Dear Rachel,
All is lost, Jesus is dead. This morning he was executed by the Roman authorities and with him die all our hopes and dreams.

Only last Sunday our hopes were high and we were so sure that the Kingdom was near. Jesus came riding into Jerusalem on an ass, his disciples following him, and all his friends from Galilee came out to welcome him. Oh Rachel, how happy you would have been to see him; all the children were dancing and singing, and the grown-ups tore branches from the palm trees and cast them before him crying: 'Hosanna! Blessed is he that cometh in the name of the Lord.'

The next day Jesus went to the temple and almost caused a riot. He overthrew the tables of the money-changers and drove out those thieves who sell doves and animals for the sacrifices. We thought this was the moment: we were sure that after cleansing the temple he would lead us to the Governor's palace and by his mighty power overthrow Pilate and the Romans. But do you know what he did? He left Jerusalem and went back to his friends in Bethany. He left, and we were all so excited that we were ready to storm Pilate's palace and face the Roman legions. But Jesus went back to Bethany.

Perhaps if Jesus had done something then he might have been alive today. Even now, after we have seen him die, we find it hard to believe that everything is finished.

I didn't know that Jesus had been arrested until I saw the crowds this morning. They were outside the Governor's palace chanting and shouting: 'Crucify him. Crucify him.' I crushed my way through to see what was happening and I can only pray to God he will help me forget what I saw. It was Jesus.

Do you remember how Jesus used to smile at us? Not with his lips and eyes like other people, but with his whole face so that it radiated peace, love, tenderness and compassion, and all the virtues we do not have. It was Jesus there, but no smile. His face was bruised, and blood was trickling down from a crown of thorns that had been placed on his head; a robe had been flung round his shoulders and blood from his scourged back was seeping through, dying it deep red. They were leading him away to crucify him.

So everything is finished, Rachel. He was not the Messiah, he was not the Son of God as Peter thought. He was just a man like us, a good man, but only human, and he is dead.

We will stay in Jerusalem until after the Sabbath day, and will travel back to Emmaus on Sunday. We will give you all the news then.

Yours, heartbroken and lost,
Cleopas

(See Luke 24 for the story of the journey back to Emmaus.)

15   Memo to Gabriel — First Easter

The Prince of Glory, in the form of the Son of man, is about to do battle with the Prince of Darkness. While we can only watch from the heavens there are certain tasks that must be done. These are as follows:

1 Arrangements must be made for angels to be available to comfort and help the Prince who will be in great distress in the Garden of Gethsemane.
2 Before the final battle commences there must be at least twelve legions of angels standing by, armed with all the necessary powers, ready to go to the aid of the Prince should he call for help.
3 After the conflict, when the Prince has died, angels must watch over the tomb.
4 At the appointed hour, angels must be in and outside the tomb where the dead body of the Prince will be laid. They alone will witness his rising from the dead. They will roll away the stone that seals the tomb.

5 Two angels will remain at the empty tomb. Women will come to anoint the body and they are to be told that the Prince has risen from the dead.

6 When the Prince ascends back into glory two angels must appear to the disciples who will witness the ascension. They will advise them that the Prince will return at the appointed time to take up his inheritance.

7 Heavenwide celebrations and rejoicings will be organised for the returning victorious Prince. Correction — he will be no longer Prince but King; all authority in heaven and earth will be given into his hands. He will reign forever as King of kings and Lord of lords.

16   The Love of God

God is love. But what does that mean? How do we know God is love? Where do we see it?

We see it in Jesus Christ.

For God so loved the world that he gave his only son!

But what does that mean?

It means Jesus left the riches of heaven for the poverty of a stable.

It means Jesus laid aside his divine power and took upon himself the weakness of man.

He laid aside his glory and humbled himself, even to death.

Supremely we see the love of God in the suffering and death of Jesus.

We see the love of God in Gethsemane.

For in the Garden of Gethsemane we see his agony and tears.

We see him setting his face resolutely to the cross.

Making his Father's will his own, that he should suffer and die.

And he suffered — for us.
We see the love of God at Gabatha, the judgment seat of
     Pilate.
There we see him silent before false accusations.
There we see him mocked.
Flogged.
Humiliated.
And he suffered for us.
We see the love of God at Golgotha, the place of
     execution.
There we see a cross.
With cruel nails.
And agonising torment of body and soul.
On the cross he was made sin — for us.
On the cross he was separated from his Father.
On the cross he endured desolation.
Darkness.
Death.
And he died — for us.

Lest I forget Gethsemane,
Lest I forget thine agony,
Lest I forget thy thorn crowned brow,
Lead me to Calvary.

17   What is Faith?

What is faith?
It is not something that saves us.
We are saved on the basis of the finished work of Christ
     upon the cross.
But faith is the means by which we lay hold of the
     salvation Christ has won.

Faith is empty hands stretched out to receive the gift of
   God.
Faith is the fundamental characteristic of a Christian.
By faith the just shall live.
Faith is not doubting — but believing.
It is not a vague hope — but a solid conviction.
It is not fear — but confidence.
It is not distrust — but steadfast living.
It is not shrinking back — but going forth boldly.
Faith is trusting Christ — and not myself.
'Faith is being sure of what we hope for and certain of
   what we do not see.' (Heb 11:1)

18   Looking at the Cross

In evil long I took delight,
   Unawed by shame or fear,
Till a new object struck my sight,
   And stopped my wild career,
I saw one hanging on a tree,
   In agonies and blood,
Who fixed his languid eyes on me,
   As near his cross I stood.

Sure, never till my latest breath
   Can I forget that look;
It seemed to charge me with his death,
   Though not a word he spoke.
My conscience felt and owned the guilt,
   And plunged me in despair;
I saw my sins his blood had spilt,
   And helped to nail him there.

Alas! I knew not what I did:
    But now my tears are vain;
Where shall my trembling soul be hid?
    For I the Lord have slain.
A second look he gave, which said,
    'I freely all forgive;
This blood is for thy ransom paid,
    I die that thou mayst live.'

Thus while his death my sin displays
    In all its blackest hues;
Such is the mystery of grace,
    It seals my pardon too.
With pleasing grief and mournful joy
    My spirit now is filled,
That I should such a life destroy,
    Yet live by him I killed.

John Newton

19   I heard the Voice

I heard the voice of Jesus say,
  'Come unto me and rest;
Lay down, thou weary one, lay down
  Thy head upon my breast.'
I came to Jesus as I was,
  Weary, and worn, and sad;
I found in him a resting-place,
  And he has made me glad.

I heard the voice of Jesus say,
  'Behold, I freely give
The living water; thirsty one,
  Stoop down and drink, and live.'
I came to Jesus, and I drank
  Of that life-giving stream;
My thirst was quenched, my soul revived,
  And now I live in him.

I heard the voice of Jesus say,
  'I am this dark world's Light;
Look unto me, thy morn shall rise,
  And all thy day be bright.'
I looked to Jesus, and I found
  In him my star, my sun;
And in that light of life I'll walk,
  Till travelling days are done.

Horatius Bonar

IV
RESPONSES TO THE
OFFER OF LIFE

1   What Does God Require?

What does the Lord require of you?
  He requires you to: seek him,
  Call upon him,
  Bow the knee,
  As creature before the Creator,
  And as sinner before the Saviour,
  He requires you to: have faith,
  Confess your sin,
  Repent of your sin,
  And then confess Christ as Saviour and Lord.
  Deny yourself,
  Take up the cross,
  And follow him.
What does God require of you?
  He requires you to: obey his Word.
  Walk in his way.
  Love God with all your heart,
  All your mind,
  All your soul,
  And all your strength,
  And your neighbour as yourself.
  He requires you to: feed the hungry,
  Give a drink to those who thirst.
  Welcome the stranger,
  Give clothes to the refugee,
  Care for the sick,
  Visit the prisoner.
What does the Lord require of you?
  To act justly.
  And to love mercy.
  And to walk humbly with your God.

2   Invitation of Jesus

Jesus calls us: by thy mercies,
  Saviour, make us hear thy call,
Give our hearts to thy obedience,
  Serve and love thee best of all.

Augustine said: 'I have read in Plato and Cicero sayings that are very wise and very beautiful. But I have never read in either of them: "Come unto me all ye that labour and are heavy laden." '

Jesus said: 'Come, follow me.' (Matt 4:19)

'Here I am! I stand at the door and knock. If anyone hears my voice and opens the door, I will go in and eat with him, and he with me.' (Rev 3:20)

'Come, follow me...and I will make you fishers of men.' (Matt 4:19)

'Trust in God; trust also in me.' (John 14:1)

'If a man is thirsty, let him come to me and drink. Whoever believes in me...streams of living water will flow from within him.' (John 7:37-38)

'He who comes to me will never go hungry.' (John 6:35)

I heard the voice of Jesus say,
  'I am this dark world's light;
Look unto me, thy morn shall rise
  And all thy days be bright.'

I looked to Jesus and I found
  In him my star, my sun;
And in that life of light I'll walk,
  Till travelling days are done.
                    (Horatius Bonar)

Just as I am, without one plea,
  But that thy blood was shed for me,
And that thou bid'st me come to thee,
  O Lamb of God, I come. (Charlotte Elliot)

3 If You Love Me

Jesus said: 'If anyone loves me, he will obey my teaching.'
(John 14:23)
  But what are the commandments of Jesus?
He said: 'You must be born again.' (John 3:7)
  'Trust in God; trust also in me.' (John 14:1)
  'Remain in me...apart from me you can do nothing.'
(John 15:4-5)
  'If anyone would come after me, he must deny himself
and take up his cross and follow me.' (Mark 8:34)
  'Unless your righteousness surpasses that of the
Pharisees...you will certainly not enter the kingdom of
heaven.' (Matt 5:20)
  'Be perfect, therefore, as your heavenly Father is
perfect.' (Matt 5:48)
  'If someone strikes you on the right cheek, turn to him
the other also.' (Matt 5:39)
  'And if someone wants to sue you and take your tunic,
let him have your cloak as well.' (Matt 5:40)
  'Do not store up for yourselves treasures on earth.'
(Matt 6:19)
  'But store up for yourselves treasures in heaven.' (Matt
6:20)
  'Do not worry about your life, what you will eat or
drink; or about your body, what you will wear.' (Matt
6:25)
  'But seek first his kingdom and his righteousness, and

all these things will be given to you as well.' (Matt
6:33)

'Do not judge, or you too will be judged.' (Matt 7:1)

'A new commandment I give you: Love one another.
As I have loved you, so you must love one another.'
(John 13:34)

'My command is this: Love each other as I have loved
you.' (John 15:12)

'Love your enemies and pray for those who persecute
you.' (Matt 5:44)

'Go and make disciples of all nations...' (Matt 28:19)

'...Teaching them to obey everything I have
commanded you?' (Matt 28:20)

'Why do you call me, "Lord, Lord" and do not do
what I say.' (Luke 6:46)

Jesus said: 'If anyone loves me he will obey my
commandments.'

4   But did Christ Die for this?

God demonstrates his own love for us in this: 'while we
were still sinners, Christ died for us.' (Rom 5:8)

If I live a good decent life — what more can God want?
   But did Christ die on Golgotha for this?
   I go to church fairly regularly.
   I'm as good a Christian as the next person without
going near a church.
   But did Christ die on Golgotha for this?
   They should make the church more attractive.
   Yes — less preaching, and more entertaining things.
   More socials.
   Concerts.

Dances.
Bingo.
Discos.
But did Christ die on Golgotha for this?
I live a decent life — what more can God want?
I've never done anybody any harm!
I'm as good as the next person!
I don't see how God can have anything against me.
But did Christ die on Golgotha for this?
What's needed is less preaching and more action.
Getting involved in social work instead of Bible study.
Getting into politics instead of prayer.
But did Christ die on Golgotha for this?

5 What will You do with Jesus?

It was Pilate the judge who asked the decisive question: 'What shall I do with Jesus?' We have all to face this question. So what will you do with Jesus?

Reject him?
Accept him?
Ignore him?
Listen to him?
Mock him?
Crown him?
Hate him?
Love him?
Use his name as a swear word?
Or as a whispered prayer?
Acknowledge his claims once a year at Christmas?
Or serve him day by day?

Treat his claims with apathy?
Or take him seriously?
Deny him?
Stand for him?
Betray him?
Follow him?
Refuse him?
Worship him?
Resist him?
Trust him?
Crucify him?
Crown him?

6   Two Roads

Life is made up of choices: little choices and big choices.
Each day we face many choices. But ultimately all the
little choices are moulded by the basic choice:
    Between right and wrong.
    Truth and error.
    Between good and evil.
    The kingdom of light and kingdom of darkness.
    Between God and Satan.
    Moses said: 'Whoever is for the Lord, come to me.'
(Exod 32:26)
    'I have set before you life and death, blessings and
curses. Now choose life, so that you and your children
may live and that you may love the Lord your God, listen
to his voice, and hold fast to him.' (Deut 30:19-20)
    Joshua said: 'Now fear the Lord and serve him with all
faithfulness...But if serving the Lord seems undesirable to
you, then choose for yourselves this day whom you will

serve...But as for me and my household, we will serve the Lord.' (Josh 24:14-15)

Elijah said: 'How much longer will it take you to make up your minds? If the Lord is God, worship him; but if Baal is God, worship him!' (1 Kings 18:21 GNB)

Jesus challenged the Church: 'I know your deeds, that you are neither cold nor hot. I wish you were either one or the other!' (Rev 3:15)

Jesus taught there are only two gates:
Narrow and wide.
Two gates leading to two roads:
Hard and easy.
Two roads trodden by two crowds:
Few and many.
Two gates, two roads, two crowds, and two destinations:
Life and destruction.

(*Cf* Matt 7:13)

7 Response to Jesus

The promises of God were fulfilled. All the wonderful promises of God — a virgin did conceive; a Son was born in Bethlehem of David's line. And his name was called Jesus for he would save his people from their sin. But what happened?

He was in the world, and the world was made by him, and the world knew him not. (John 1:10 AV)

He came unto his own, and his own received him not. (John 1:11 AV)

He was laid in a manger because there was no room for him in the inn. (*Cf* Luke 2:7)

King Herod sought to kill him. (*Cf* Matt 2:16)

The foxes had holes, the birds of the air had nests, but Jesus, the Son of man, had nowhere to lay his head (*Cf* Matt 8:20)

All spoke well of him and were amazed at the gracious words that came from his lips. 'Isn't this Joseph's son?' they asked. (Luke 4:22)

But some religious teachers said 'Why does this fellow talk like that? He's blaspheming! No one can forgive sins but God alone'. (*Cf* Mark 2:7)

A crowd took up stones to stone him. (*Cf* John 8:59)

Many of his disciples turned back and no longer followed him. (John 6:66)

Judas betrayed him with a kiss. (*Cf* Luke 22:48)

Three times Peter denied even knowing him. (*Cf* John 18:17-26)

Then all the disciples deserted him and fled. (Matt 26:56)

With one voice the crowd cried out, 'Away with this man.' (*Cf* Luke 23:18)

Then they spat in his face and struck him with their fists. Others slapped him and said, 'Prophesy to us, Christ. Who hit you?' (Matt 26:67-68)

Pilate tried to wash his hands of him. (*Cf* Matt 27:24)

But the crowd shouted all the louder, 'Crucify him!' (*Cf* Mark 15:14)

And when they had mocked him, they took off the purple robe and put his own clothes on him. Then they led him out to crucify him. (Mark 15:20)

He was in the world, and though the world was made through him, the world did not recognise him. (John 1:10)

He came unto his own, and his own received him not. (John 1:11 AV)

8   Who will Stand and Speak for Jesus?

At this moment war, terrorism, crime, violence, vandalism, hate and death ravish our world.
  Who will stand and speak for Jesus?
At this moment children are dying of starvation. Politicians argue, statesmen attend conferences, we throw ten per cent of our food away, and thousands die daily.
  Who will stand and speak for Jesus?
At this moment men are lying in prison because of the colour of their skin. Men are in prison or awaiting execution because of the principles of their hearts.
  Who will stand and speak for Jesus?
At this moment young people of our country indulge in glue sniffing, smoking marijuana, or injecting heroin into their veins. Destroying their life in a search for living.
  Who will stand and speak for Jesus?
At this moment lounge bars are crowded. There the name of the Saviour is a thoughtless curse or an idle oath. 'Jesus Christ', they say, and the name is drowned in drunken laughter.
  Who will stand and speak for Jesus?
At this moment clubs and cabarets are crowded. In the alcoholic haze, smutty jokes and loud noise drives away all thoughts of the love or claims of God.
  Who will stand and speak for Jesus?
At this moment many people are members of the Church; looking upon it as a social club, a good, an interesting, a respectable place to go. Faithful on a Sunday, forgetful the rest of the week.
  Who will stand and speak for Jesus?
At this moment we live in an age that is lost. We live in a world of sin and rebellion, apathy and indifference. We live among a people who need the gospel, who need faith, hope and love.

Who will stand and speak for Jesus?

And I heard the voice of the Lord saying: 'Whom shall I send? And who will go for us?'

9   Whom shall I Send?

A long time ago God confronted Isaiah and said: 'Whom shall I send? And who will go for us?' (Isa 6:8)

And Jesus said: 'As the Father has sent me, I am sending you.' (John 20:21)

Today God calls you to be his messengers.

Do you hear?

Do you go?

He wants people to go to China.

Africa.

South America.

And into all the world.

Do you hear?

Do you go?

He wants to send people into pulpits.

On to platforms.

Into the open air.

Do you hear?

Do you go?

He wants to send you to your family.

Your neighbours.

Your friends and workmates.

Do you hear?

Do you go?

God doesn't call us all to be preachers, teachers, pastors or evangelists.

But we are all called to be his witnesses.

We are all called to give evidence of his love and saving Gospel.

We are all called to be able to give a reason for our faith.

We are Christ's ambassadors.

We are commissioned.

Do we obey?

Do we go?

God says today: 'Whom shall I send? And who will go for us?'

10   The Word of the Prophet

Amos 4:6-12 reads in the Authorised Version:

6 And I also have given you cleanness of teeth in all your cities, and want of bread in all your places: yet have ye not returned unto me, saith the Lord.

7 And also I have withholden the rain from you, when there were yet three months to the harvest: and I caused it to rain upon one city...one piece was rained upon, and the piece whereupon it rained not withered.

8 So two or three cities wandered unto one city, to drink water; but they were not satisfied: yet have ye not returned unto me, saith the Lord.

9 I have smitten you with blasting and mildew: when your gardens and your vineyards and your fig trees and your olive trees increased, the palmerworm devoured them: yet have ye not returned unto me, saith the Lord.

10 I have sent among you the pestilence after the manner of Egypt: your young men have I slain with the sword, and have taken away your horses; and I have made the stink of your camps to come up into your nostrils: yet have ye not returned unto me, saith the Lord.

11 I have overthrown some of you, as God overthrew

Sodom and Gomorrah, and ye were as a firebrand plucked out of the burning: yet have ye not returned unto me, saith the Lord.
12 Therefore thus will I do unto thee, O Israel: and because I will do this unto thee, prepare to meet thy God, O Israel.

Beautiful language, poetic and sad, and yet it sounds so hopelessly out of date. What does it mean to us today? Supposing — just supposing — a prophet like Amos came to us today. What would he say? What would his message be to us, the children of the late 20th century?

O land, beloved of the Lord. Why will you not listen? Hear the Word that comes to this self-satisfied, self-deceiving generation. Thus says the Lord. Behold I gave you wars and military disasters with hordes of evil conquering Europe. Men fought on the land, in the air, on the seas and even in the waters under the seas. Your cities were laid waste and death and destruction rained down on the heads of your defenceless people.

Yet you have not returned unto me, says the Lord.

I brought peace to the land and it came to pass that you faced the long years of austerity with food rationing, scarcity and shortages. In it, all of you dreamed great dreams of the world you would build with the strength of your own hands.

Yet you did not return unto me, says the Lord.

In the years of peace you found there was no peace. Your young men were taken from you to die in Korea, Malaya, Burma, Cyprus, Egypt, Aden, Northern Ireland and the Falkland Islands.

Yet you have not returned unto me, says the Lord.

Behold I gave you the years of affluence with full employment and money for all. Lo, you had cars and money in the bank. You had new homes with every luxury, television and videos, long hours of leisure and holidays abroad. Your young were educated freely, your sick were cared for without money or without price, and the aged and those unable to work were given that which ensured none would starve. But behold in the years of affluence you became puffed up with pride and declared 'Lo, we have never had it so good.'

Yet you have not returned unto me, says the Lord.

Now your currency has been devalued. Inflation and economic recession has fallen like a blight on the land so that poverty is the lot of many. Your youths and young maidens protest and riot; violence and vandalism darkens your cities, and hope for a bright shining future now lies dying on your litter-strewn streets.

Yet you have not returned unto me, says the Lord.

Now, amid the desolation of the age, you search for pleasure among the things that cannot satisfy. You seek forgetfulness in alcohol and drugs. You glory in seeing sex and violence portrayed on your cinema and television screens and love the language of the gutter in your plays, films and entertainment. And in the search for money for which you will not work the cry of 'Bingo' is heard in the land.

Yet you have not returned unto me, says the Lord.

Therefore, thus says the Lord: 'I come and bring

judgment unto you. So prepare to meet your God, O Great Britain!'

11   Forgetfulness

Moses warned Israel: 'Be careful that you do not forget the Lord your God, failing to observe his commands, his laws and decrees.' (Deut 8:11)

But we have short memories, haven't we?

We do forget.

We forget that God made the world.

We forget it is he who gives sunshine and rain.

It is he who set the stars in their courses.

We forget that we are creatures made by God.

Dependent upon God.

We forget that everyone we meet bears the image of God.

We forget the commandments of God.

Such as having nothing at the centre of our lives — but God alone.

Such as worshipping with God's people every week.

We forget to read his word regularly.

And to pray daily.

We forget the Christian heritage that is ours.

The freedom of worship that was bought at a price.

We forget that men died to bring us the Bible in a language we can understand.

We forget that democracy was worked out under God.

We forget that the welfare state grew out of Christian concern.

That individual freedom came from Christian influences.

That science and education flourished on a biblical basis.

'Be careful to forget not the Lord your God.'
But we have short memories.
We do forget the love of God the Father.
We do forget the grace of God the Son.
We do forget the fellowship of God the Spirit.

NB: Read Psalm 103:1-5

12   This is not a Thankful Age

We do not live in a truly thankful age. Think of the things for which we should be thankful.

Think of the wonderful creation in which we live.
The life-giving sun and the cool light of the moon.
The twinkling stars against the blackness of space.
Snow-capped mountain peaks.
And fertile valleys.
With rivers and streams.
Waterfalls and rapids.
Trees and flowers in a myriad of colours.
Singing birds.
Vast oceans and inland seas.
Are we thankful?
Think of the simple necessities of life we enjoy.
Homes to live in.
Clothes to wear.
Food when we're hungry.
Water when we're thirsty.
A bed when we're tired.
Are we thankful?

Think of the lives we live.
Books and magazines to read.
Music to enchant.
Games to play.
Places to go.
Jokes to laugh at.
Are we thankful?
Think of the relationships we have.
With parents.
And children.
Brothers and sisters.
Husbands and wives.
Friends and colleagues.
Are we thankful?
Think of the spiritual blessings we have.
A Father God who loves us.
A brother who died for us.
A Holy Spirit who comforts and guides us.
And a home where we will all meet together in the end.
Are we thankful?

13   What's your Excuse?

Jesus confronts us and calls us to follow him. But few take
up the challenge. Many do nothing. And they have lots of
excuses. What's your excuse?

People will think I'm mad.
    I don't want to be the odd one out.
    I don't want to be thought a fanatic.
    I'm good enough without Jesus.
    I'm as good as the next person.
    I've never done anyone any harm.

I don't think I need religion.
Nobody goes to church nowadays.
It's not relevant to me.
It's a lot of nonsense.
It's old fashioned.
It's for middle-class hypocrites.
It's for old people and children.
It's not convenient just now.
I can't make up my mind.
It will cost too much.
There's plenty of time.
I'm too busy.
And God said: 'You fool'. (Luke 12:20)

14   When Jesus came to —

When Jesus came to Bethlehem
   They left him in the cold,
There was no place within the inn
   The finest rooms were sold;
All the palaces were crowded,
   The homes were full of light,
But Mary and the little child
   Were left out in the night.

When Jesus came to Scotland
   We'd learned a thing or two;
Yet still we could not welcome him
   We had so much to do;
We had the Christmas cards to write,
   The parcels all to send,
The Christmas tree to decorate
   And money more to spend.

So when Jesus came to our town
   For his work is never done,
We had no time to welcome him
   We wanted so much fun:
So in our whirl of Christmas cheer
   The Lord wished he was able
To go back to Bethlehem
   And the comfort of the stable.

15   An Honest Hymn

Take my life and let it be
   Partly given, Lord, to thee;
Take my moments and Sundays,
   I will give an hour of praise.

Take my hands and let them move
   Sometimes in response to love;
Take my feet and let them be
   Swift in action, all for me.

Take my voice and let me sing
   Every Sunday for my King;
Take my lips that they may be
   Filled with talk — about me.

All my silver and my gold,
   Most of it I will withhold;
Take my intellect for use
   In every way I should choose.

Don't take my will, it is mine
  I don't want to make it thine;
And my heart, it is mine own
  Lord I keep it for my throne.

Take my love, my Lord, I pour,
  At weekly worship all its store;
Take myself and I will be
  Maybe, sometimes, Lord, for thee.

16   Why will Ye Die?

Sinners, turn; why will ye die?
  God, your maker, asks you why;
God, who did your being give,
  Made you with himself to live;
He the fatal cause demands,
  Asks the work of his own hands:
Why, ye thankless creatures, why
  Will ye cross his love, and die?

Sinners, turn; why will ye die?
  God, your Saviour, asks you why;
God, who did your souls retrieve,
  Died himself, that ye might live.
Will ye let him die in vain?
  Crucify your Lord again?
Why, ye ransomed sinners, why
  Will ye slight his grace, and die?

Sinners, turn; why will ye die?
  God, the Spirit, asks you why;
He, who all your lives hath strove.

Wooed you to embrace his love;
Will ye not his grace receive?
Will ye still refuse to live?
Why, ye long-sought sinners, why
Will ye grieve your God, and die?

Charles Wesley

V
THE LIFE JESUS OFFERS

1   The Answer is

In spite of men's opinions and in answer to their despair, there is the promise of God; the facts of the Gospel. But it's much easier to go our own way. It's much more comfortable to decide that God doesn't exist, or at least is remote from our personal life. It seems clever to be trendy, to think we're progressive, educated, sophisticated in our thinking. But down through history when men have tried to go it alone they've come up against the realities of life. And without God, despair is the only road to walk.

But the answer is: there is a God.
God made the world.
Face the facts: man fell.
There is sin in the world.
I'm a sinner.
You're a sinner.
Face the facts: God loves the world.
God loves me.
God loves you.
The answer is: God sent his son into the world.
Face the facts: Christ was born of the Virgin Mary.
Suffered under Pontius Pilate.
Was crucified.
Dead and buried.
Face the facts: the answer is — he rose again.
And is now seated at the right hand of God.
From whence he shall come to judge the living and the dead.
Face the facts: Jesus is alive.
Pilate is dead.

Caesar is dead.
Jesus is alive.
The answer is: we are sinners.
But God loves us.
Christ died for us.
And by his Spirit we can be made new.
Are you prepared to turn to him?

2   What is a Christian?

What is a Christian?
   A Christian is one who knows he is a sinner and trusts
in Christ for salvation.
   He is a sinner, saved by grace.
   He realises some religious knowledge is not enough.
   But has trusted his life to Jesus.
   He realises some attempt to be good is not enough.
   But trusts the goodness of Jesus.
   He realises that no amount of religious observance is
enough.
   Such as regular church attendance.
   Daily Bible reading.
   And nightly prayers.
   He knows that only Christ can save.
   The Christian is a realist who lives in the real world —
because the real world is God's.
   The Christian is the person who can say:

>   Not the labour of my hands
>   Can fulfil thy law's demands:
>   Could my zeal no respite know,
>   Could my tears for ever flow,
>   All for sin could not atone,

Thou must save, and thou alone.
Nothing in my hands I bring,
Simply to thy cross I cling.

A Toplady

3   To Decide for Jesus

To decide for Jesus — what does it mean?
It means:
Forgiveness.
Peace.
Satisfaction.
Contentment.
Patience.
Happiness.
Life.
Liberty.
Fulfilment.
Freedom.
Purity.
Holiness.
Humility.
Self-control.
Love.
Hope.
Grace.
Joy.
Power.
Victory.
And it can also mean:
Frustration.
Pain.

Sorrow.
Tears.
A cross.
Death.
But above and beyond all things, it means:
Life.
Real life.
Abundant life.
Eternal life.
Real life.
Life.

4   What is a Disciple?

What is a disciple?
   Someone who has trusted Christ.
   Who worships God.
   Seeks to know him better.
   To serve him in all things.
   And to be his witness in the world.
What is a disciple?
   A follower of Jesus.
   A child of God.
   One who worships God in spirit and in truth.
   With love and devotion.
What is a disciple?
   A student in the school of Christ.
   One who seeks to learn more about Jesus.
   And know the power of his resurrection.
   And the fellowship of his sufferings.
   Becoming like him.
What is a disciple?
   A servant of God.

An obedient servant.
A steward of God.
A soldier of Christ.
Who cares for others.
Loves and shares with others.
What is a disciple?
One sent into the world.
To be the salt of the earth.
And the light of the world.
To witness to God's saving grace.
What is a disciple?
It is someone who has trusted Christ.
And is pure.
Peace-loving.
Considerate.
Submissive.
Full of mercy.
And good fruit.
Impartial.
And sincere.

(*Cf* James 3:17)

5   What God Thinks of Us

What does God think of us?
He said: 'Let us make man in our image.'
So we are reflections of God.
We are his workmanship.
Made higher than the angels.
Only a little lower than God himself.
We are his vice-regents on earth.
To rule and have dominion and subdue the earth.

We are the image-bearers of God.
But man fell.
God sees us as sinners.
Falling short of his glory.
Breaking his law.
As sheep who have gone astray.
We are lost.
Disobedient.
Rebellious.
Unfaithful.
Everyone has gone their own way.
And our righteousnesses are as filthy rags in his sight.
God sees us as sinners, needing salvation.
What does God think of us?
He thinks we are worth loving.
Worth sending his son to redeem us.
Worth dying for.
Worth adopting into his family.
Worth making us heirs of his glory.
What does God think of us?
He sees us as his creation.
He sees us in rebellion against him.
And longs for us to turn to him.

6   Hope

What is hope?
Is it — something to warm our disappointments?
Is it — vain dreams?
Empty wishes?
Wild longings?
Is hope a wish of fancy, unrelated to reality?
Is it — the vain desire of a heart?

Are your hopes beyond reach?

Are your hopes ever shattered?

It is hard to find hope in a hopeless age.

One writer asks: 'Is there hope in a time of abandonment?'

Another says that we can only have: 'a blind and empty
   hope in the pit of despair'.

Yet man cannot live without hope.

Where can hope be found?

Politics?

Economics?

Technology?

Sociology?

Planning?

Science?

Education?

But these are the gods that have already failed.

Where can hope be found?

In God.

The God of hope.

In God's word.

The word of hope.

Such hope is well grounded.

It is a solid conviction.

The future is God's.

The Christian hope rests in Almighty God.

In God's promises.

In God's word.

In God's Son.

It is a living hope through the resurrection of Jesus Christ
   from the dead. (*Cf* 1 Peter 1:3)

7　Happiness

What is happiness?
It's having money to spend.
It's having possessions to enjoy.
It's being successful.
It's having a sense of security.
It's having a job.
Job satisfaction.
Happiness is a good marriage.
A loving family.
Children.
Grandchildren.
It's having friends.
Being well thought of.
Happiness is when things go well.
Good health.
A night out.
Our team winning.
But happiness is deeper than these things.
For it is knowing God cares.
Knowing God loves.
It is trusting God.
Knowing he will provide for all our needs.
Knowing that all things work for our good if we love him.
Happiness is abiding in Christ.
Obeying God's Spirit.
And obeying his word.
As Moses said: 'Happy are you people, who are saved by
the Lord.' (*Cf* Deut 33:29)

8   The Fruit of the Spirit

The fruit of the Spirit is:
Love.
Joy.
Peace.
Patience.
Kindness.
Goodness.
Faithfulness.
Gentleness.
Self-control.
This is to be the character of the Christian.
You are to grow into people like this.
It doesn't happen overnight.
But are you growing?
It is the fruit of the Holy Spirit — not you.
Are you allowing the Divine Gardener to work in your
    life?
Or are you grieving him?
The fruit of the Spirit is:
Love towards God.
Joy under all circumstances.
Peace amid conflict.
Patience with people who try you.
Kindness towards those who don't deserve it.
Goodness in the midst of evil.
Faithfulness in an age of doubt.
Gentleness in an age of ruthlessness.
Self-control in an age of indulgence.

9   What Faith Gains

We are saved by grace — through faith. Christ is therefore the basis of salvation, and faith is the key to open the door to Christ's offer.

By faith we obtain salvation.
Eternal Life.
The Kingdom of God.
Heaven.
By faith we are justified.
Made righteous.
Our guilt removed.
By faith we are sanctified.
We obtain the fulness of the Holy Spirit.
We obtain provision for our every need.
We overcome the world.
By faith we triumph over all opposition.
By faith we have access to God.
By faith we claim the promises of God.
By faith we receive the peace of God.
By faith we receive the joy of Christ.
By faith we walk with God.
Enter into the family of God.
Become partakers in a worldwide community.
By faith we are in Christ.
And nothing can separate us from the love of God.

10   What is a Christian Family?

What is a family?
It is a God-given institution for the benefit of man.

For God says: 'I have set the lonely in families.'
And the family gives stability to society.
But today there is a breakdown of the family.
And we need to return to God's standard for the family.
Today we need real families.
Christian families.
But what is a Christian family?
It is a family which worships God.
It is a family which knows Christ — not as a guest — but
   as Lord.
It is a family which is guided by God's word.
It is a family which worships together day by day.
And enjoys life together.
Which prays together.
And plays together.
Which has time for God.
And for one another.
Which grows together — in love for God.
And for one another.
A Christian family, is part of God's wider family on earth
   and in heaven.

11   Lord of All

Abraham Kuyper — minister of God's word, journalist,
editor, university professor, economist, sociologist,
politician, and Prime Minister of Holland 1901-1905 said:
'There is not one square inch of human life over which
Christ does not say, "I am King." '

We say: 'You are my Lord and King.'
   Except all the things I feel I want to do.
   Except all the things I like to do.

Christ is Lord of my life — except when I am planning my holidays.

Except what I do with my spare time.

Except how I spend my money.

Christ is Lord of my life — except in my daily work.

Except in my relationships.

There is not one square inch of my life over which Christ does not say: 'I am King.'

I agree — except the books I read.

The newspapers I buy.

The television programmes I watch.

Except all the bits and pieces of my life that I want to keep for myself.

Let us pray:

Let us pray:

'Lord, you are King.'

'But Lord — you know I don't live that out.'

'Lord, you are King.'

'But Lord, I don't find it easy to follow you.'

'Lord, you are King.'

'But Lord, I am continually letting you down. I find it hard to be your obedient servant.'

'Lord, you are King.'

'Yes Lord — I know there is not one square inch of my life over which you do not say, "I am King." Help me to remember this and try to live it out.'

12   You Reap what You Sow

'Do not be deceived: God cannot be mocked. A man reaps what he sows.' (Gal 6:7)

What do we sow today?
And what are we reaping?

We sow with only a thought to the short-term interest.
And reap long-term confusion.

We sow for material gain.
And we reap spiritual poverty.

We sow for pleasure.
And we reap destructive self-centredness.

We sow to selfishness.
And we reap dissatisfaction.

We sow to pride.
And we reap a fall.

We sow moral permissiveness.
And we reap disease and anarchy.

We sow to our lusts.
And we reap the degradation of human values.

We sow deceit.
And we reap distrust.

We sow to a religion that is half-hearted, cosy and comfortable.
And we reap an ineffective Church, with a faith that is irrelevant to the world.

'Do not be deceived: God cannot be mocked. A man reaps what he sows.'
What are you sowing?

13   Testimony of Jeremiah

Jeremiah was a prophet who lived long ago and far away. Have you ever wondered what men like him would say if they came back today? Supposing we could hear the testimony of Jeremiah. What would he say to us? What would he tell us? Maybe it would be something like this:

I am Jeremiah, son of Hilkiah, who was one of the priests at Anathoth in the territory of Benjamin. And the Lord appointed me as a prophet to the nations. It was a long time ago now so it must be hard for you to understand the age and times in which I lived. How can you understand it? It must surely be beyond all your imaginings. Your age and culture must be so very different from my own.

I lived among a generation of men and women who had left the God of their fathers. They deliberately left God out of their thinking, out of their actions and out of their lives. Is not that beyond all understanding? Has any other nation ever changed its gods? But that is exactly what my nation and people did; they changed their gods. They exchanged the glory and service of the living God for worthless idols. And you know what happened. They became worthless themselves. A worthless people worshipping worthless idols.

There were a few of us who held to the true and living God. We tried, we pleaded and begged, yes, even with tears, for the people to turn to the Almighty One. To trust him alone. To read his word and walk in his ways. And we warned of the dangers of judgment in disobedience to God's law. But they would not listen. They were not interested.

Of course there was no shortage of popular prophets, preachers and politicians telling them everything was all right. 'Peace' — that was the great cry. 'Peace'. The people wanted peace but they wanted a peace without God. Can you imagine it? All the false prophets and cult preachers and publicity-seeking politicians kept telling people just to trust them and follow their ways. Then they would have peace and progress.

And God became a stranger in the land. How can you understand such a terrible thing happening?

A people who did not know God, who never read his word, who did not pray or praise the God who had created all things. Yet they could see his works all around them. They saw the autumn and spring rains but felt that it had nothing to do wth God. They saw the seasons as simply a matter of meteorological science; just part of some laws of nature established by some evolutionary process. So they took pride in their wisdom and were proud of their own riches and strength. And God was a stranger in the land.

The little children knew no Bible stories; those of mature age seldom, if ever, entered a church, and the aged had forgotten the meaning of worship. Such a thing happening to a nation must be strange to your ears. But it happened in my times and to my generation.

My people loved to wander in their own ways, doing their own things, and forgot about God and his love and his laws. I told them, I pleaded with them, to stand at the crossroads and look; to ask for the old ways, the ways of the living God—but they would not listen. They would not walk in the ways of the Lord.

It drove me to tears, hot burning tears. I remember longing that my head might be a spring of water so that I might weep night and day for my people.

It was a sad time. It must be hard for you to understand such a time. Surely if you had lived in such an age as mine it would have driven you to tears. Surely you too would have wept for a lost generation that knew

E

not God, that did not want to know him, and was fervently searching for a peace and satisfaction that only he could give.

Yes, it must be hard for you to imagine or understand the age and times in which I lived.

14   Letter from Elijah

At the height of success the prophet Elijah broke communion with God and fled from a wrathful Queen Jezebel. Journeying into the desert he sat down in deep depression under a bush. What were his feelings? He might have written to his faithful servant like this:

Greetings from a weary soul. I am going far into the desert, heavy of heart and low in spirit. I am sorry, beloved friend, but I am depressed and despondent, weary of life and tired of everything. I wish I had never been born and can now only long to die.

'Is this not Elijah, the prophet of the living God?' you will say. But am I not also a man? I am tired of it all. The dead barrenness of the desert will suit the emptiness of my mind as I go to escape and forget. Do not lose faith, beloved friend. There is still a God, great and almighty, who can do great and mighty things. We saw him. Remember Mount Carmel? The false prophets built a fire for their sacrifice but their false gods could not light the wood. But our God sent fire from heaven to burn the sacrifice and confound his enemies.

Then there was the drought. God withheld the rain because I had prayed and sent the rain back in answer to my prayer. Seven times you went up to see if the rains were coming and your faith must have been sorely tried.

But how your heart must have lifted when you saw a cloud, no bigger than a man's hand, but it was Almighty God, answering the prayer of his servant.

So do not lose faith. I have not lost faith. I know and believe there is still the living God.

But I have failed. My life's work has come to nothing. These people will not listen. They still worship false gods and run after false prophets. They still have Ahab and Jezebel — but I am too tired even to speak of the loathing in my heart for them. I am nothing and I have failed. These people will never turn to God. They don't want him. I, only I, am left. So I am dejected and discouraged; life is a weariness and the future is dark and dreary. I long for death, for the angel of death to carry me away.

So I will go into the desert and ask the Lord to take my life from me. There is nothing left and I am alone.

(*Two new voices*)

Then he went into a cave and spent the night. And the word of the Lord came:

'What are you doing here, Elijah?'

He replied: 'I have been very zealous for the Lord God Almighty. The Israelites have rejected your covenant, broken down your altars, and put your prophets to death with the sword. I am the only one left and now they are trying to kill me too.'

The Lord said: 'Go out and stand on the mountain in the presence of the Lord, for the Lord is about to pass by.'

Then a great and powerful wind tore the mountain apart and shattered the rocks before the Lord, but the Lord was not in the wind. After the wind there was an earthquake, but the Lord was not in the earthquake. After the earthquake came a fire, but the Lord was not in the fire. After the fire came a gentle whisper. When

Elijah heard it, he pulled his cloak over his face and went out and stood at the mouth of the cave.

The Lord said to him: 'Go back the way you came...I reserve seven thousand in Israel all whose knees have not bowed down to Baal and all whose mouths have not kissed him.'

(*Cf* 1 Kings 19:9ff)

15   Thy Way — Not Mine

Thy way, not mine, O Lord,
　However dark it be!
Lead me by thine own hand,
　Choose out the path for me.

Smooth let it be or rough,
　It will be still the best;
Winding or straight, it leads
　Right onward to thy rest.

I dare not choose my lot;
　I would not, if I might;
Choose thou for me, my God;
　So shall I walk aright.

The kingdom that I seek
　Is thine; so let the way
That leads to it be thine;
　Else I must surely stray.

Take thou my cup, and it
　With joy or sorrow fill,
As best to thee may seem;
　Choose thou my good and ill;

Choose thou for me my friends,
　My sickness or my health;
Choose thou my cares for me,
　My poverty or wealth.

Not mine, not mine the choice,
　In things or great or small;
Be thou my guide, my strength,
　My wisdom, and my all!

Horatius Bonar

VI
RESOURCES OF LIFE

1   What is the Bible?

Whatever way you look at it, the Bible is an astonishing book. It is totally unlike any other book that has ever been published. In fact it is more than a book — it is a library of 66 books. But consider these facts:

It was written over a period of 1600 years.
It was written in three languages: Hebrew, Aramaic and Greek.
It was written in three continents: Asia, Africa and Europe.
It contains a rich diversity of literature:
History
Doctrine.
Poetry.
Biography.
Letters.
Proverbs.
Law.
Truth and grace.
It was written by over 40 authors from every walk of life.
There was Moses, a great political leader trained in the universities of Egypt.
There was Peter, a fisherman.
Amos, a herdsman.
Joshua, a military general.
Daniel, a prime minister.
Luke, a doctor.
Solomon, a king.
Matthew, a tax collector.

David, a shepherd who became a king.

Paul, an intellectual.

Samuel, a prophet.

And it was written in many different places.

Moses wrote in the wilderness.

Paul wrote in prison.

Daniel in a palace.

Jeremiah in a dungeon.

Luke while travelling.

Joshua and David in the midst of military campaigns.

John while an exile on the Isle of Patmos.

The Bible is an astonishing book, quite unlike any other book because ultimately, behind all the men who wrote, there is one author.

All Scripture is inspired by God.

And is useful for teaching the truth.

Rebuking error.

Correcting faults.

And giving instruction for right living. (*Cf* 2 Tim 3:16 GNB)

Ultimately only the Scriptures are able to give us the wisdom that leads to salvation in Christ Jesus.

Listen to what the Bible claims for itself.

Jesus said: 'The Scripture cannot be broken.' (John 10:35)

Above all, you must understand that no prophecy of Scripture came about by the prophet's own interpretation. For prophecy never had its origin in the will of man, but men spoke from God as they were carried along by the Holy Spirit. (2 Peter 1:20)

For everything that was written in the past was written to teach us, so that through endurance and the encouragement of the Scriptures we might have hope. (Rom 15:4)

Jesus said: 'Heaven and earth will pass away, but my words will never pass away.' (Matt 24:35)

The Psalmist said: 'Your word, O Lord, is eternal; it stands firm in the heavens.' (Ps 119:89)

Jesus said: 'Do not think I have come to abolish the Law or the Prophets; I have not come to abolish them but to fulfil them. I tell you the truth, until heaven and earth disappear, not the smallest letter, not the least stroke of a pen will by any means disappear from the Law until everything is accomplished.' (Matt 5:17-18)

God's word is truth.
The law of the Lord is perfect;
Reviving the soul.
The statutes of the Lord are trustworthy;
Making wise the simple.
The precepts of the Lord are right;
Giving joy to the heart.
The commands of the Lord are radiant;
Giving light to the eyes.
The fear of the Lord is pure;
Enduring for ever.
The ordinances of the Lord are sure;
And altogether righteous.
They are more precious than gold.
Than much pure gold.
They are sweeter than honey.
Than the honey from the comb.
By them is your servant warned.
In keeping them there is great reward. (*Cf* Ps 19:7-11)

All Scripture is God-breathed and is useful for teaching, rebuking, correcting and training in righteousness, so that the man of God may be thoroughly equipped for every good work. (2 Tim 3:16)

2   What Men Say About the Bible

The Bible has survived the passing years; it has survived intense scrutiny and criticism. The Psalmist said: 'Your word is a lamp to my feet and a light for my path.' But let us listen to what others have said about the Bible. (Ps 119:105)

Thomas Watson, a Puritan, wrote: 'Read the Scripture, not only as history, but as a love-letter sent to you from God.'

The first American President, George Washington, said: 'Above all, the pure light of revelation has had an influence on mankind, and increased the blessings of society. It is impossible rightly to govern the world without God and the Bible.'

Thomas Jefferson, another US President, said: 'I have always said that a studious perusal of the sacred volume will make better citizens, better fathers and better husbands.'

William Gladstone, a British Statesman, said: 'I have known 95 of the world's great men in my time, and of these, 87 were followers of the Bible.'

Lord Tennyson wrote: 'Bible reading is an education in itself.'

Immanuel Kant, one of the greatest of all philosophers, wrote: 'The existence of the Bible, as a book for the people, is the greatest benefit which the human race has ever experienced. Every attempt to belittle it is a crime against society.'

Henry Ward Beecher, the American novelist, said: 'Sink the Bible to the bottom of the ocean, and man's obligations to God would be unchanged. He would have the same path to tread, only his lamp and guide would be gone; he would have the same voyage to make, only his compass and chart would be overboard.'

Josh Billings wrote: 'Almost any fool can prove the Bible ain't so — it takes a wise man to believe it.'

Someone noted: 'Men do not reject the Bible because it contradicts itself but because it contradicts them.'

Cecil B De Mille, the film producer, wrote: 'After more than 60 years of almost daily reading of the Bible, I never fail to find it always new and marvellously in tune with the changing needs of every day.'

John Flavel, a Puritan, said: 'The Scriptures teach us the best way of living, the noblest way of suffering, and the most comfortable way of dying.'

The great explorer and missionary, David Livingstone, confessed: 'All that I am I owe to Jesus Christ, revealed to me in his divine Book.'

John Locke, a great philosopher, wrote: 'The Bible is one of the greatest blessings bestowed by God on the children of men — it has God for its author, salvation for its end, and truth without mixture for its matter. It is all pure, all sincere; nothing too much; nothing wanting.'

Someone wrote: 'Other books were given for our information, the Bible was given for our transformation.'

Sir Isaac Newton, one of the greatest of our scientists,

wrote: 'We account the Scriptures of God to be the most sublime philosophy. I find more sure marks of authority in the Bible than in any profane history whatever...No sciences are better attested than the religion of the Bible.'

David Nygren writes: 'If all the neglected Bibles were dusted simultaneously, we would have a record dust storm and the sun would go into eclipse for a whole week.'

Sir Walter Scott wrote:
> Within that awful volume lies
> the mystery of mysteries!
> Happiest they of human race,
> To whom God has granted grace
> To read, to fear, to hope, to pray,
> To lift the latch, and force the way:
> And better had they ne'er been born,
> Who read to doubt, or read to scorn.

Mark Twain wrote: 'Most people are bothered by those passages in Scripture which they cannot understand; but as for me, I always noticed that the passages in Scripture which troubled me most are those which I do understand.'

Queen Victoria said: 'The Bible is the secret of England's greatness.'

Isaac Watts wrote:
> The stars, that in their courses roll,
> Have much instruction given;
> But thy good word informs the soul
> How I may climb to heaven.

NB: In presenting this script it is advisable to use only a selection of the quotations.

3   The Bible Survives

From a purely human point of view it is astonishing we still have a Bible to read. Down through the centuries many have tried to destroy and banish the Bible from the face of the earth. It has been attacked by atheists, by unbelievers, by ruthless dictators, false philosophers, and by 'science, falsely so called'. It has been burned, and those found reading it executed. But all efforts to destroy the Bible have failed. All attacks have left it stronger than ever. It is an anvil that has worn out many hammers.

In AD 303 the Roman Emperor issued an edict that all Christians should be killed and their sacred book destroyed. Churches were razed to the ground and thousands of Christians martyred. Throughout the Empire many thousand Bibles were publicly burned and the Emperor rejoiced that 'the name of the Christians has perished from the earth.'

Yet within 25 years, Constantine was Emperor of Rome and he was a Christian. Indeed he commissioned Bibles to be copied at the expense of the government.

Voltaire was the great French sceptic of the 18th century. He mocked the Church and Christian faith and claimed that within 100 years Christianity would be swept out of existence and the Bible a forgotten book.

Yet within 50 years of his death, Voltaire's house and printing press were being used by the Geneva Bible Society to produce and store Bibles for distribution throughout Europe.

In our own century, Lenin boasted that religion would wither and die and the Bible no longer be needed or heeded. In the Russian revolution of 1917 the churches were closed, the buildings turned over to anti-God museums, the Bible was banned and atheism taught in all the schools.

Yet, after over 60 years of atheistic propaganda, with the Bible almost unobtainable, the Church is thriving and growing in Russia. Three times over in the past ten years the Russian government has allowed the Bible Societies to import Bibles into their country, and recently in response to public demand they allowed Bibles to be printed in Russia itself.

China followed Lenin, closing the churches and banning the Bible.

Yet now the churches are being reopened and crowds of believers are flocking back to worship God.

People are clamouring for Bibles — the book Diocletian, Voltaire and Lenin thought would be forgotten and lost!

4   The Promises of Jesus

Jesus promises many things. And these can be ours as we take him at his word and lay hold of what he has promised.

Jesus promises: forgiveness for our sin.
To take our guilt away.
And make us new creatures.
To create within us a new heart.
Jesus promises: fellowship with himself if we will open our lives to him and let him in.
Jesus promises: 'I will be with you always.'
Jesus promises: to give us peace.

Real peace which is peace of heart and mind and soul.
Jesus promises: to give us joy.
The joy of forgiven sin.
The joy of fellowship with him.
Jesus promises: to give us rest.
A refuge in the storms of life.
Jesus promises: to give us courage.
'Be of good cheer,' he said, 'for I have overcome the
    world.'
Jesus promises us the Holy Spirit.
To comfort us.
To teach us.
To guide us.
Jesus promises us the Kingdom of Heaven.
Jesus promises us many things.
If we will come with the empty hands of faith — they
    are ours.

5 What Jesus Says

Jesus taught many things. Listen to some of his claims and
promises.

Anyone who has seen me, has seen the Father.
    I and the Father are one.
    I have come down from heaven, to do the will of him
who sent me.
    No one comes to the Father except through me.
    I am the way and the truth and the life.
    I am the true vine, and my Father is the gardener.
    I am the gate, whoever enters through me will be
saved.
    I am the good shepherd.

The good shepherd lays down his life for the sheep.

I am the bread of life, he who comes to me will never go hungry, and he who believes in me will never be thirsty.

I am the resurrection and the life. He who believes in me will live, even though he dies.

I am the light of the world, whoever follows me will never walk in darkness.

I tell you the truth, before Abraham was born — I am!

Do not let your hearts be troubled, trust in God, trust also in me.

Peace I leave with you, my peace I give you.

Come to me, all you who are weary and burdened, and I will give you rest.

Jesus read from Isaiah: 'The spirit of the Lord is on me because he has anointed me to preach good news to the poor. He has sent me to proclaim freedom for the prisoners and recovery of sight for the blind, to release the oppressed, to proclaim the year of the Lord's favour.' (Isa 61:1-2)

Then he continued: 'Today this Scripture is fulfilled in your hearing.'

For God so loved the world that he gave his one and only son, that whoever believes in him shall not perish, but have eternal life.

Jesus said: 'All authority in heaven and in earth has been given to me.'

6 What is Prayer?

What is prayer?
It is many things.
It is praise,
Telling God how great he is.

It is worship and adoration,
Acknowledging that God alone is worthy to be
worshipped.

It is confession,
Admitting that we have fallen short of God's standards,
and are sorry.

It is petition,
Telling God the things we think we need.

It is thanksgiving,
Giving God thanks for all he has done and is doing for us.

It is intercession,
Bringing the needs of others to God.

What is prayer?
It is seeking God's will.
It is having a conversation with God.
Talking to God.
And listening to him as well.

What is prayer?
It is the creature in living communication with the
Creator.
And the child talking to his Father.

7   What Men Say about Prayer

Listen to what preachers, writers, statesmen have said about prayer.

E M Bounds said: 'Prayer is the contact of a living soul with God. In prayer, God stoops to kiss man, to bless man, and to aid in everything that God devises or man can need.'

C H Spurgeon said: 'Prayer is the slender nerve that moves the muscles of omnipotence.'

E M Bounds said: 'Prayer is the language of a man burdened with a sense of need. Not to pray is not only to declare that there is nothing needed, but to admit to a non-realisation of that need.'

John Bunyan said: 'The best prayers have often more groans than words.'

V L Crawford said: 'Prayer is the spiritual gymnasium in which we exercise and practise Godliness.'

Thomas Fuller said: 'Prayer should be the key of the day and the lock of the night.'

Someone said: 'We are to ask with a beggar's humility, to seek with a servant's carefulness, and to knock with the confidence of a friend.'

R W Dale said: 'Work without prayer is atheism; and prayer without work is presumption.'

Robert Murray McCheyne said: 'If I could hear Christ praying for me in the next room, I would not fear a million enemies. Yet distance makes no difference. He is praying for me.'

Someone said: 'If Christians spent as much time praying as they do grumbling, they would soon have nothing to grumble about.'

Benjamin Franklin said: 'Work as if you were to live 100 years; pray as if you were to die tomorrow.'

John Keble said: 'And help us, this and every day, to live more nearly as we pray.'

Abraham Lincoln said: 'I have been driven many times to my knees by the overwhelming conviction that I had nowhere else to go.'

Shakespeare said: 'My words fly up, my thoughts remain below. Words without thoughts never to heaven go.'

C H Spurgeon said: 'If religion is not a farce with some congregations, at any rate they turn out better to see a farce than to unite in prayer.'

H E Fosdick said: 'God is not a cosmic bell-boy for whom we can press a button to get things.'

A Hebrew proverb runs: 'God does not listen to the prayers of the proud.'

Jean Ingelow said: 'I have lived to thank God that all of my prayers have not been answered.'

A Jewish proverb runs: 'Every man wants to pray the day before he dies. As he does not know when his time will come, he must pray every day in order to be safe.'

James Montgomery wrote:

> Prayer is the soul's sincere desire,
> Uttered or unexpressed,
> The motion of a hidden fire
> That trembles in the breast.
>
> Prayer is the burden of a sigh,
> The falling of a tear,
> The upward glancing of an eye
> When none but God is near.

NB: In presenting this script it is advisable to use only a selection of the quotations.

8   What is Grace?

What is grace?
It is the undeserved favour of God.
It is the mercy and love of God.
It is the winsome attractiveness of God.
It means the strength of God to overcome.

> Amazing grace! How sweet the sound
> That saved a wretch like me;
> I once was lost, but now am found;
> Was blind, but now I see.

Grace is God coming to sinners.
Appealing to sinners — 'Come to me!'
Grace is Christ nailed to a cross.
A Christ bearing the sin of the world.
A Christ condemned — for me.

Grace is the outstretched hands of a loving Father.
Waiting to welcome the wanderer home.

> Through many dangers, toils and snares
> I have already come
> 'Tis grace that brought me safe thus far,
> And grace will lead me home.

Grace is God with us in the storms of life.
God's protection and guidance day by day.
It is God's daily provision.
God's peace in our heart.
And a hope that can never fail.

> Yes, when this heart and flesh shall fail,
> And mortal life shall cease,
> I shall possess within the veil
> A life of joy and peace.

John Newton

9 What is the Church?

What is the Church?
It is a community of worship.
Of obedience.
Of fellowship.
Of service.
Of care.
Of faith.
Of hope.
It is a community of love.
The Church is the Kingdom of God.

The family of God.
The people of God.
The army of God.
The building of God.
The flock of God.
The children of God.
The Church — is the Church of God.
The Church is — the body of Christ.
The bride of Christ.
Of which Jesus said: 'I will build my Church and the gates
   of hell will not overcome it.'
The Church is called by the Spirit of God.
Guided by the Spirit of God.
Equipped by the Spirit of God.
The Church is people who are indwelt by the Spirit of
   God.
The Church is a chosen people.
A holy nation.
A royal priesthood.
Living stones.
A people called to show forth his praise.
A people called to be the salt of the earth.
And the light of the world.
The Church is a people bound together by the word of
   God.
By the love of God.
By love one for the other.
And service to God and others.
The Church is a people who actually bring glory to
   God.

10   The Sacraments

Among the gifts God has given the Church are the sacraments, which remind us of the spiritual truths at the heart of our faith.

There is the sacrament of baptism.

In baptism we are reminded that we are sinners.

Guilty before God.

Under the judgment of God.

Spiritually dead before God.

But that in Christ we are forgiven.

Brought into the family of God by faith in Jesus.

And through faith receive eternal life.

There is the sacrament of the Lord's Supper.

In the Lord's Supper we are drawn in memory to what God has done for us.

To the Christ on the cross — suffering and dying for us.

Here we remember his death for us.

Here we remind ourselves of the need to feed our souls by faith day by day.

One day these signs and symbols will have passed away.

And we will be with him.

And we shall be like him for we shall see him as he is.

11   Preaching the Word

One of the great resources for living that God has been
pleased to give us is the preaching of his word.

For in that word we receive:
The illumination of God.
We learn of God.
And of ourselves with our needs.
We learn of the character of God.
His holiness.
Love.
Justice.
Mercy.
In the preaching of his word we hear the Gospel.
With its offer of salvation.
And its call to faith.
In the preaching of his word our souls are fed.
As we hear of the Christian faith.
The Christian hope.
The Christian love.
The comfort of the Christian.
The challenge to the Christian.
The way of the Christian.
In the preaching of his word we encounter that Word
    which is a lamp to our feet and a light to our path.
In the preaching of his word we encounter the living word
    — Jesus.

12   What is Prayer?

Prayer is the soul's sincere desire,
    Uttered or unexpressed;
The motion of a hidden fire
    That trembles in the breast.

Prayer is the burden of a sigh,
    The falling of a tear,
The upward glancing of an eye,
    When none but God is near.

Prayer is the simplest form of speech
    That infant's lips can try;
Prayer is the sublimest strains that reach
    The Majesty on high.

Prayer is the contrite sinner's voice,
    Returning from his ways;
While angels in their songs rejoice,
    And cry, 'Behold, he prays!'

Prayer is the Christian's vital breath,
    The Christian's native air,
His watchword at the gates of death:
    He enters heaven with prayer.

The saints in prayer appear as one
    In word and deed and mind,
While with the Father and the Son
    Sweet fellowship they find.

Nor prayer is made by man alone,
　　The Holy Spirit pleads,
And Jesus on the eternal throne
　　For sinners intercedes.

O thou by whom we come to God,
　　The Life, the Truth, the Way!
The path of prayer thyself hast trod:
　　Lord, teach us how to pray!

James Montgomery

13   Watch and Pray

The God that stopped the sun on high
　And sent the manna from the sky,
Laid flat the walls of Jericho,
　And put to flight old Israel's foe;
Why can't he answer prayer today,
　And drive each stormy cloud away?

Who turned the water into wine,
　And healed a helpless cripple's spine,
Commanded tempest, 'Peace, be still,'
　And hungry multitudes did fill;
His power is just the same today,
　So why not labour, watch and pray?

He conquered in the lions' den,
　Brought Lazarus back to life again,
He heard Elijah's cry for rain,
　And freed the sufferers from pain.
If he could do those wonders then,
　Let's prove our mighty God again.

Why can't the God who raised the dead,
　Gave little David Goliath's head,
Cast out the demons with a word,
　Yet sees the fall of one wee bird,
Do signs and miracles today,
　In that same, good, old-fashioned way?
He can! He's just the same today!

Martin Luther

14   God's Unchanging Word

For feelings come and feelings go,
And feelings are deceiving;
My warrant is the word of God,
Naught else is worth believing.
Though all my heart should feel condemned
For want of some sweet token,
There is one greater than my heart
Whose word cannot be broken.
I'll trust in God's unchanging word
Till soul and body ever;
For, though all things shall pass away,
His word shall stand forever.

Martin Luther

15   Exhortation to Prayer

What various hindrances we meet
In coming to a mercy-seat!
Yet who, that knows the worth of prayer,
But wishes to be often there?

Prayer makes the darkened cloud withdraw;
Prayer climbs the ladder Jacob saw,
Gives exercise to faith and love,
Brings every blessing from above.

Restraining prayer, we cease to fight;
Prayer makes the Christian's armour bright;
And Satan trembles when he sees
The weakest saint upon his knees.

While Moses stood with arms spread wide,
Success was found on Israel's side;
But when thro' weariness they failed,
That moment Amalek prevailed.

Have you no words? Ah! think again,
Words flow apace when you complain,
And fill your fellow-creature's ear,
With the sad tale of all your care.
Were half the breath, thus vainly spent,
To Heaven in supplication sent,
Your cheerful song would oftener be,
'Hear what the Lord has done for me!'

William Cowper